microwave cooking library™

microwaving poultry & seafood

by barbara methven

microwave cooking library™

As Americans consume less red meat, the popularity of poultry and seafood increases. Consumers recognize poultry and seafood as excellent sources of lean, highly nutritious protein, at comparatively moderate cost per serving. They are also among the foods the microwave oven cooks best.

If you haven't been using your microwave oven to prepare poultry and seafood, you're missing one of its major benefits. These foods microwave tender and juicy, with a delicious flavor that can be either delicate or robust.

Microwaving Poultry & Seafood provides information on how to select quality products and cook them creatively. Four pages of comprehensive charts offer detailed instructions for defrosting or cooking the varieties and cuts of poultry and seafood which are generally available nationwide.

Generously illustrated with color photographs and step-by-step directions, the book includes recipes for appetizers, soups and stews, salads and sandwiches, tempting main dishes, even special sauces. If you're an enthusiastic microwave cook of poultry and seafood, you'll welcome this store of new recipes. If you aren't, this book will help you become one.

Barbara Methven

Barbara Methven

CREDITS:
Design & Production: Cy DeCosse Incorporated
Senior Art Directors: Sue Schultz, Bill Nelson
Art Director: Lynne Dolan
Project Managers: Sue Kersten, Mary O'Brien
Production Consultant: Christine Watkins
Production Manager: Jim Bindas
Assistant Production Manager: Julie Churchill
Typesetting: Jennie Smith, Bryan Trandem
Production Staff: Michelle Alexander, Yelena Konrardy, Linda Schloegel, Nik Wogstad
Photographers: Tony Kubat, Jerry Robb, Kris Boom, Jerry Krause
Food Stylists: Susan Zechmann, Suzanne Finley, Lynn Lohmann, Susan Sinon, Lynn Bachman
Home Economists: Jill Crum, Peggy Lamb, Kathy Weber
Recipe Editor: Myrna Shaw
Color Separations: La Cromolito
Printing: Moebius Printing Company

Additional volumes in the Microwave Cooking Library series are available from the publisher:

- Basic Microwaving
- Recipe Conversion for Microwave
- Microwaving Meats
- Microwave Baking & Desserts
- Microwaving Meals in 30 Minutes
- Microwaving on a Diet
- Microwaving Fruits & Vegetables
- Microwaving Convenience Foods
- Microwaving for Holidays & Parties
- Microwaving for One & Two
- The Microwave & Freezer
- 101 Microwaving Secrets
- Microwaving Light & Healthy

CY DE COSSE INCORPORATED
Chairman: Cy DeCosse
President: James B. Maus
Executive Vice President: William B. Jones

Library of Congress Cataloging-in-Publication Data.

Microwaving Poultry & Seafood.

(Microwave Cooking Library)
Includes index. 1. Microwave Cookery. 2. Cookery (Poultry) 3. Cookery (Seafood) I. Title. II. Title: Microwaving Poultry and Seafood. III. Series: Methven, Barbara. Microwave Cooking Library.
TX832.M4155   1986   641.6'65   85-29382
ISBN 0-86573-516-6

Published by Prentice Hall Press
A Division of Simon & Schuster, Inc., New York
ISBN 0-671-62268-4

Contents

What You Need to Know Before You Start

Microwave cooking is a superlative way of preparing many types of poultry, fish and shellfish. Poultry remains succulent without basting. Seafood cooks briefly in its own natural juices, which brings out the delicate flavor and achieves a flaky but firm texture.

Because microwave cooking intensifies flavors, it is important to start with high quality, strictly fresh poultry and seafood. Use fresh products the same day you buy them, or the following day. Poultry and seafood from your freezer can be defrosted just prior to cooking to prevent loss of juices, which begin to seep as soon as the ice crystals have melted.

Many cooks believe that microwaved seafood tastes less 'fishy' than conventionally cooked seafood. You may notice a fishy odor when defrosting or microwaving some types of seafood, especially shrimp, but this odor usually disappears immediately after cooking.

Choosing Poultry for Microwaving

The poultry recipes in this book have been developed with types of poultry for which microwaving offers a distinct advantage in flavor, texture or cooking time.

A small turkey or a plump broiler-fryer are excellent choices for microwaving, and are preferable to roasting chickens or capons, which have less tender skin.

A few items are better cooked conventionally. These are stewing hens, which need long, slow cooking to tenderize; geese, which brown in the microwave oven but do not achieve a crisp skin; and turkeys weighing more than 11 pounds.

Using the Fish Recipes

There are hundreds of varieties of saltwater and freshwater fish. To compound the complexity, the same fish may have different names in different regions. Some varieties are seasonal, while others are found only in limited localities.

This book has been written for use across the continent, using fish and shellfish which are generally available. Several varieties of fish may be substituted in most recipes. If you are fortunate enough to obtain fresh local species, you can use the recipes in this book by selecting one for a fish which is similar in size and thickness to your local variety.

The fat content of fish is less important when microwaving than when cooking by conventional methods, some of which may dry out or toughen lean fish. In microwave cooking, thick or fatty fish are cooked at a lower power level and may be rotated more often. This reduces the possibility of 'popping,' which can occur when heat builds up in a fatty area. Popping does not dry out the fish or affect its flavor.

Poultry

Fresh poultry is available in a variety of forms to suit any family size. In addition to whole or quartered chickens, you can select all white or all dark meat to suit your preference. Turkey is no longer reserved for holidays or large groups. Smaller birds and turkey parts make it economical, everyday family fare.

In some parts of the country, poultry is shipped frozen, and is thawed at the market by tempering, a process of slow defrosting at very low temperatures, which inhibits the growth of bacteria. This poultry can be refrozen at home, if it is done immediately after purchase. The danger from thawed and refrozen poultry comes from meat which has thawed at room temperature; this encourages the growth of bacteria.

When defrosting poultry at home, use your microwave oven. For minimal loss of juices, defrost poultry just before cooking. If you must hold it after defrosting, refrigerate it until cooking time.

How Much Poultry to Buy

Most poultry is excellent and relatively low-cost protein. The cost per serving is determined by the ratio of meat to bone, plus the amount of fat. Broiler-fryers weighing over 2½ lbs. have a better meat to bone ratio than smaller birds. Even if your family is too small to use the heavier chicken at one meal, you can freeze part of it, plan a second meal using leftover chicken, or buy a small package of chicken parts from meatier birds.

When buying turkey, allow ¾ to 1 lb. per serving. The maximum size for microwaved turkey is 10 to 11 lbs. Larger birds should be roasted conventionally.

Boneless turkey parts, such as cutlets or tenderloins, serve four persons per pound. Bone-in turkey breast makes two to three servings per pound, while meaty thighs serve two persons per pound. If you plan to combine the meat with other ingredients for a casserole or salad, you'll need less turkey per serving.

When buying Cornish hens, allow one bird per person. Ducklings are very bony and fatty. A 4 to 5-lb. bird serves two to four people, depending upon appetites.

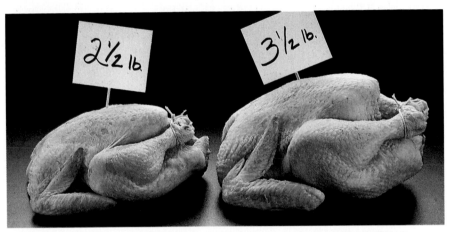

Compare a 2½-lb. broiler-fryer, which serves four, with a 3½-lb. fryer serving six. That extra pound provides enough meat for 2 more servings. A 1½-lb. broiler-fryer only serves two.

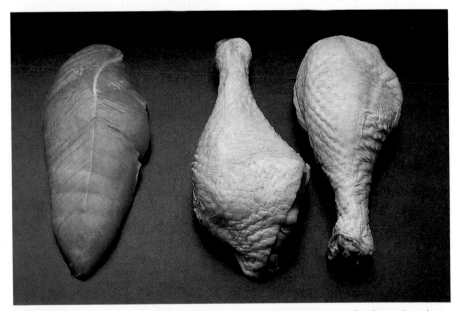

Consider cost per serving rather than cost per pound when buying turkey parts. The per pound cost of boneless tenderloins is over six times greater than turkey legs, but the serving cost is only twice as much because legs contain so much bone.

How to Select Fresh Chicken

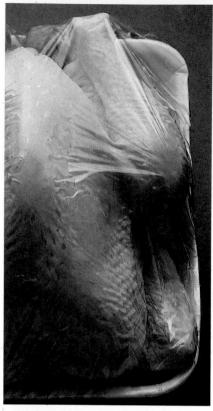
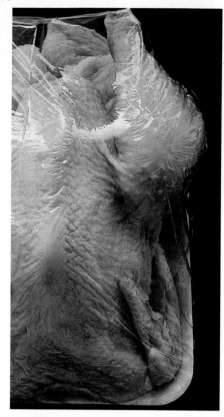
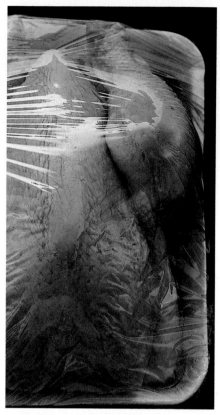

Choose plump broiler-fryers weighing at least 2½ lbs. Look for smooth skin and minimum of moisture in package.

Avoid stewing hens and fryers with thick skin, large pores or excess fat under the skin.

Check for large amounts of pink liquid in bag. This may indicate that chicken has been frozen.

How to Select Frozen Poultry

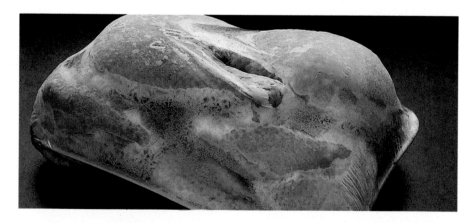

Inspect package for tears, which cause freezer burn. Avoid packages which contain pink ice. This indicates that poultry was thawed and has been refrozen. It will be less juicy.

How to Store Poultry

Poultry is very perishable. Store chicken in the original package and use it the day you buy it. If you wish to keep it until the following day, wash it in water, pat dry and wrap in plastic wrap or a clean, dry plastic bag.

Fresh turkey and turkey parts may be refrigerated up to 2 days in the original package. Ground turkey and turkey breakfast sausage are shipped frozen. If your market has thawed them for sale, use within 24 hours.

Knowing how to cut up poultry is a useful art. A whole chicken may cost less per pound than a cut-up bird, and can be disjointed at home. Quartered chickens will microwave more evenly if they are cut into eight pieces. Use a heavy, well-sharpened chef's knife, and cut through the joints rather than the bone. The back and trimmings can be used for stock.

How to Prepare Chicken for Cooking

Wash chicken in water and remove excess fat. Pat dry.

Skin chicken for low-fat preparation. Most of the fat is in, or directly under, the skin. In conventional cooking, skinned chicken may stick to the pan or dry out in cooking. Microwave cooking eliminates these problems.

How to Freeze Poultry

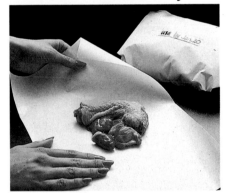

Remove giblets and freeze separately if you plan to keep poultry longer than 3 months. Giblets will not keep as long as the rest of the bird.

Freeze chicken or turkey parts in original package if you will use it within 2 weeks.

Overwrap package with freezer foil for longer storage, or remove poultry from package and wrap in coated freezer paper.

How to Test Poultry for Doneness

Whole birds are done when legs move freely at joint and flesh feels very soft to pressure. Juices run clear when breast meat under wing and inner thigh is pierced with a skewer. Internal temperature of turkeys should be 170-180°F. on a quick-read thermometer. Do not roast with temperature probe.

Poultry parts are done when meat near bone is no longer pink. Juices from boneless cuts should run clear.

Fish

As Americans become more conscious of changes in nutritional recommendations, they are eating more fish. Both saltwater and freshwater fish provide excellent protein with relatively little waste.

There was a time when fresh fish were a dietary staple for people who lived beside rivers, lakes or seas, while just a few miles inland, the only fish available were smoked, pickled, salted or canned. Today, preserved fish are enjoyed for their unique characteristics or convenience, but modern methods of catching, refrigerating and transporting fish make a greater variety of fresh seafood available across the continent.

Use Fish Promptly

Fish are very perishable. If they are to be sold fresh, they must be flown from coastal processing centers to the point of sale. The quality of fresh fish depends on whether they were gutted before icing, how quickly they were iced after catching, and how much time has elapsed in transporting them from ship to supermarket. For best results, cook fresh fish the day you buy it, or on the following day.

Some markets defrost fish for sale by tempering, a method of slow defrosting at very low temperatures, or by setting packages out in a refrigerated meat case. Fish defrosted at very cold temperatures will keep as long as fresh, but will lose texture and quality if they are refrozen.

Store fish in the coldest part of the refrigerator, covered with plastic wrap.

Know Your Frozen Fish

Improvements in freezing techniques have led to greater quality and variety in frozen fish. Some fishing fleets which work far out to sea freeze the fish as they are brought aboard. Many producers now freeze fillets, steaks or pan-dressed fish individually, encased in a thin glaze of ice which helps retain moisture.

If you are buying fish for the freezer, your wisest choice is to buy already frozen fish. This eliminates the possibility that you may be refreezing thawed fish. Fish which are flash-frozen immediately after catching will have a fresher taste and texture than fish which are home-frozen after they have been in storage several days. Use your microwave oven to defrost frozen fish just before cooking.

How to Select Fresh Fish

Look for moist, translucent flesh when buying fillets or steaks. Dry or milky surface indicates age.

Press whole or dressed fish lightly with finger. Flesh should be firm and springy.

Check for shiny, firmly adhering scales and fresh, non-fishy odor. Fresh whole fish have bulging eyes and reddish gills.

How to Select and Store Frozen Fish

How to Test for Doneness

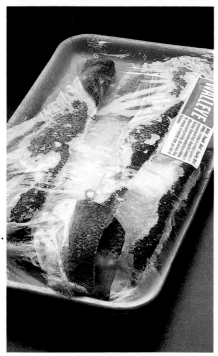

Avoid packages with torn wrappings. These result in freezer burn. Pink ice in package indicates fish has thawed and been refrozen; it may be spoiled.

Store in a freestanding freezer at 0°F or below, if possible. Fish kept in a frost-free compartment should be used within two or three weeks.

Microwave only until fish flakes easily with fork. Flesh will be just barely opaque.

How to Substitute Fish

The recipes in this book have been written for fish which are generally available across the country. Local fish may be substituted when you are fortunate enough to obtain them. Thickness of the fish is critical when you make substitutions, since microwaving time is affected by it. Fatty fish are generally microwaved at a lower power level and rotated more often than lean. The following chart lists fish called for in this book with some suggested substitutions.

Choose a recipe for fish which is similar in thickness, fat content, weight and cut to the one you wish to use. Compare large walleye fillets with orange roughy. Whole bass, perch, whiting or scup may be prepared like rainbow trout.

Fish	Fat Content	Substitutions
Catfish, freshwater	medium	Bluegill, crappie, grouper, haddock, perch, pike, pollock, sunfish
Cod	lean	Burbot, cusk, haddock, halibut, pollock, scrod, shark, whiting, wolf fish (ocean catfish)
Flounder	lean	Croaker, fluke, halibut*, orange roughy, perch, pike, scup, sole, turbot*
Grouper or Sea Bass	lean	Burbot, corbina, cusk, haddock, hake, halibut, monkfish, muskellunge, orange roughy, pike, rockfish, snapper, tilefish, whiting
Haddock	lean	Cod, flounder, orange roughy, pollock, shark, sole, wolf fish, (ocean catfish)
Halibut	lean	Grouper, haddock, hake, orange roughy, pollock, rockfish, scrod, turbot
Orange Roughy	lean	Cod, haddock, turbot, walleye
Salmon	medium to fatty	Arctic char, bluefish, dolphin (mahi mahi), mackerel, pompano, sea trout, sturgeon, swordfish, tuna
Snapper	lean	Angler, bass, drum, haddock, monkfish, orange roughy, perch, rockfish, sea trout, sheepshead
Sole	lean	Same as flounder
Trout	fatty	Bass, bluefish, butterfish, greyling, mullet, perch, pike, pompano, scup
Turbot	lean	Same as flounder

*May be thicker than flounder and sole.

Shellfish

In the past, shellfish were even less available to inland cooks than fish. Only oysters, packed in straw and ice or snow, could survive the trip inland. Even with today's air shipment, the availability of fresh shellfish is limited because all shellfish are extremely perishable. Some must be kept alive until they are used. Whether they are live or not, refrigerate fresh shellfish immediately and use them within 24 hours.

Live crab is found only in coastal markets. For shipment inland, the meat is cooked and frozen. Crab legs, as well as green shrimp and shucked oysters, scallops or clams, are often purchased frozen and then defrosted for sale by the market. Seafood sticks, which make an economical substitute for crab, are also sold defrosted. Refrigerate defrosted shellfish and use within 24 hours.

The freezer case yields a variety of shellfish, some of them caught in distant waters and available due to modern freezing techniques. While some inland markets offer live lobsters in tanks, we have limited our lobster recipes to frozen tails. Live lobsters must be killed before microwaving. Too often they are merely stunned. Conventional boiling may be a more humane method of cooking live lobster.

When selecting frozen shellfish, look for packages without tears or dents. Icy rims on boxes may indicate that the product has thawed and refrozen.

How to Select Fresh Shellfish

Make sure mussels, clams and oysters in the shell are alive. Shells should be tightly closed, or should close quickly when they are touched.

Look for shucked scallops, oysters and clams, which are sweet smelling and plump, with clear liquor.

Test shrimp and prawns for firm flesh and fresh smell. Avoid those with slimy surface or ammonia odor.

How to Clean Mussels and Clams

Scrub shells with stiff brush under cold running water to remove sand. Scrape off barnacles and snip beard from mussels.

Soak, if desired, for 3 to 4 hours, in cold solution of ⅓ cup salt to 1 gallon of spring water. Chlorinated water may harm shellfish. Cornmeal may be sprinkled over clams to help purge sand and grit.

How to Clean Shrimp

Peel back shell and legs, starting from underside at head end. Tail may be left in place, if desired.

Make shallow slit down back of shrimp.

Remove intestinal vein.

15

Defrosting &
Cooking Techniques

On the following pages you will find charts with comprehensive directions for microwave defrosting and cooking of poultry and seafood. Although individual applications differ, the basic cooking techniques are similar for poultry, fish and shellfish.

Shield vulnerable areas with foil. During defrosting, breasts and wing and leg tips of whole poultry, or the thin tail areas of whole fish may become warm and start to cook. Pieces of foil protect these spots while the rest of the bird or fish defrosts. When cooking whole poultry, shield any areas which may over-brown.

Separate pieces as soon as possible during defrosting. Poultry parts, fish fillets and bulk shellfish are often frozen in a solid mass. After an initial period of defrosting to loosen the pieces, break them apart and spread in a single layer so energy can reach them evenly.

Let stand to complete defrosting of large items like lobster tails and whole poultry. This allows temperature to equalize throughout the food.

16

Cover poultry pieces, shellfish and lean fish with a casserole lid or vented plastic wrap when steaming is desired. To hold in heat without steaming, cover chicken pieces and fatty fish, such as salmon or trout, with wax paper.

Rotate or turn in the oven whole poultry, fish, lobster tails and dishes of fillets. This avoids the build up of heat in any one spot.

Arrange pieces of poultry or seafood with thickest portions toward the outside of the dish, where they will receive more energy. Thin parts of fillets may be overlapped in the center of the dish.

Turn over or rearrange fish steaks and poultry after half the cooking time. Thin or fragile fish fillets should not be turned over; instead overlapping areas should be reversed.

Defrosting Poultry

Type	Power Level	Time	Procedure
Chicken, Whole	30% (Low)	5 to 9 min./lb.	Unwrap and place breast-side down in baking dish. Cover with wax paper. Microwave for half of time. Turn breast-side up. Shield if needed. Microwave remaining time. Remove giblets. Let stand 5 to 10 minutes until cool but not icy.
Quarters, Legs, Thighs, Wings	50% (Med.)	4 to 6½ min./lb.	Unwrap and place in baking dish or on roasting rack. Microwave for half of time. Separate pieces. Arrange with thickest portions toward outside. Microwave remaining time. Let stand 10 to 15 minutes until cool but not icy.
Boneless Breasts	50% (Med.)	5½ to 8 min./lb.	Unwrap and place in baking dish or on roasting rack. Microwave for half of time. Separate pieces. Microwave remaining time until pliable but cold. Let stand 15 to 20 minutes.
Livers	50% (Med.)	4 to 7 min./lb.	Place package in microwave oven. Microwave for half of time. Unwrap and separate livers. Microwave remaining time. Let stand 5 minutes until livers can be pierced with fork.
Turkey, Whole, bone-in, no larger than 11 lbs.	50% (Med.)	3½ to 5½ min./lb.	Estimate total defrosting time and divide into 4 parts. Unwrap and place breast-side down in baking dish. Microwave for one-fourth of total time. Turn breast-side up. Microwave for one-fourth of time. Shield warm spots as needed. Let stand 15 minutes. Turn turkey on side. Microwave for one-fourth of time. Turn turkey on other side. Microwave remaining time. Remove giblets. Let stand in cool water 30 to 60 minutes until cool but not icy.
Whole, boneless, 5 to 6 lbs.	50% (Med.)	7½ to 9½ min./lb.	Unwrap and place on roasting rack. Microwave for half of time, turning over once. Let stand 15 minutes. Remove gravy packet. Turn turkey over. Microwave remaining time, turning over once. Let stand 20 minutes until cool but not icy.
Bone-in Breast	50% (Med.)	3½ to 5½ min./lb.	Unwrap and place skin-side down on roasting rack. Microwave for half of time. Remove gravy packet. Turn skin-side up. Shield if needed. Microwave remaining time. Rinse in cool water. Let stand 5 to 10 minutes until cool but not icy.
Boneless Breast, no larger than 5 lbs.	50% (Med.)	7½ to 9½ min./lb.	Unwrap and place on roasting rack. Microwave for half of time, turning over once. Let stand 15 minutes. Remove gravy packet. Shield if needed. Turn turkey over. Microwave remaining time, turning over once. Let stand 20 minutes until cool but not icy.
Legs, Thighs, Wings	50% (Med.)	5½ to 7½ min./lb.	Unwrap and place on roasting rack. Microwave for half of time. Turn over and rearrange. Microwave remaining time. Let stand 15 minutes until cool but not icy.
Tenderloins	50% (Med.)	4 to 6 min./lb.	Unwrap and place on roasting rack. Microwave for half of time. Shield thin portions. Microwave remaining time. Let stand 10 to 15 minutes until cool but not icy.
Cutlets	30% (Low)	7 to 11 min./lb.	Unwrap and place on roasting rack. Microwave for half of time. Separate and rearrange as soon as possible. Microwave remaining time, until pliable but still icy. Let stand to complete defrosting.
Ground	50% (Med.)	4 to 6 min./lb.	Unwrap and place in casserole. Microwave, removing defrosted portions to another dish. Let stand 10 minutes.
Cornish Hens	50% (Med.)	5 to 7 min./lb.	Unwrap and place breast-side down in baking dish. Cover with wax paper. Microwave for half of time. Turn breast-side up. Shield if needed. Rearrange hens. Microwave remaining time. Remove giblets. Let stand 5 minutes.
Duckling	50% (Med.)	4½ to 6 min./lb.	Unwrap and place breast-side down in baking dish. Cover with wax paper. Microwave for half of time. Turn breast-side up. Shield if needed. Microwave remaining time. Remove giblets. Let stand 5 to 10 minutes until cool but not icy.

Microwaving Poultry

Type	Power Level	Time	Procedure
Chicken, Whole	High	5 to 8 min./lb.	Place breast-side up on roasting rack. Cover with wax paper. Microwave until legs move freely and juices run clear, rotating rack twice. Let stand, covered, 10 minutes.
Quarters, Breasts, Legs, Thighs, Wings	High	4 to 8 min./lb.	Arrange on roasting rack with thickest portions toward outside. Cover with wax paper. Microwave until no longer pink and juices run clear, rearranging once or twice. Let stand, covered, 3 minutes.
Turkey, Whole, bone-in, no larger than 11 lbs.	High first 10 min., then 50% (Med.)	12 to 15 min./lb. total time	Estimate total cooking time and divide into 4 parts. Place turkey breast-side down in baking dish. Microwave at High for 10 minutes. Reduce power to 50% (Medium). Microwave remainder of first one-fourth of time. Turn breast-side up. Shield if needed. Baste. Microwave at 50% (Medium) for one-fourth of time. Drain. Turn turkey on side. Microwave at 50% (Medium) for one-fourth of time. Turn turkey on other side. Baste. Microwave remaining time until internal temperature of thickest portion of each thigh registers 180°F. Let stand, tented with foil, 20 to 30 minutes.
Whole, boneless, 5 to 6 lbs.	High first 10 min., then 70% (Med. High)	11 to 15 min./lb. total time	Place turkey in nylon cooking bag. Secure bag loosely with string. Place in baking dish. Microwave at High for 10 minutes. Reduce power to 70% (Medium High). Microwave remaining time until internal temperature registers 175°F in several places, turning over 2 or 3 times. Let stand, tented with foil, 15 to 20 minutes.
Bone-in Breast	High first 5 min., then 50% (Med.)	12½ to 16½ min./lb. total time	Estimate total cooking time and divide into 4 parts. Place turkey skin-side down on roasting rack. Microwave at High for 5 minutes. Reduce power to 50% (Medium). Microwave remainder of first one-fourth of time. Turn turkey on side. Microwave at 50% (Medium) for one-fourth of time. Turn turkey on other side. Baste. Microwave at 50% (Medium) for one-fourth of time. Turn turkey skin-side up. Baste. Microwave remaining time until internal temperature registers 170°F. Let stand, tented with foil, 10 to 20 minutes.
Boneless Breast, no larger than 5 lbs.	High first 5 min., then 50% (Med.)	16 to 18 min./lb. total time	Place turkey on roasting rack. Microwave at High for 5 minutes. Reduce power to 50% (Medium). Microwave remaining time until internal temperature registers 170°F, turning over after half the time. Let stand, tented with foil, 10 to 20 minutes.
Legs, Thighs, Wings	70% (Med. High)	13 to 17 min./lb.	Place turkey in baking dish with ¼ cup broth or wine. Cover. Microwave until juices run clear, turning over after half the time. Let stand, covered, 5 minutes.
Ground	High	4 to 7 min./lb.	Crumble turkey into casserole. Cover. Microwave until firm and cooked through, stirring twice.
Cornish Hens	High	5½ to 8 min./lb.	Place breast-side up on roasting rack. Cover with wax paper. Microwave until legs move freely and juices run clear, rearranging once or twice. Brush with glaze. Let stand, covered, 5 minutes.
Duckling	High first 10 min., then 50% (Med.)	6½ to 9½ min./lb. total time	Estimate total cooking time and divide in half. Place duckling breast-side down on roasting rack. Secure neck skin to back with wooden picks. Microwave at High for 10 minutes. Drain. Reduce power to 50% (Medium). Microwave remainder of first half of time. Drain. Turn duckling breast-side up. Brush with glaze. Microwave at 50% (Medium) for remaining time. Drain. Brush with glaze. Let stand, tented with foil, 5 minutes.

Defrosting Fish & Shellfish

Type	Power Level	Time	Procedure
Fish, Whole, small	50% (Med.)	3½ to 6½ min./lb.	Unwrap and place in baking dish or on roasting rack. Microwave for half of time. Separate and rearrange. Shield heads and tails. Microwave remaining time until fish is pliable but icy in center. Let stand 5 to 10 minutes.
Fillets, block	50% (Med.)	6 to 10 min./lb.	Unwrap and place in baking dish or on roasting rack. Microwave for half of time. Separate fillets as soon as possible. Microwave remaining time until fish is pliable but still icy. Let stand 10 minutes.
Fillets, glazed	50% (Med.)	5 to 8 min./lb.	Unwrap and arrange on roasting rack. Microwave for half of time. Rearrange once. Microwave remaining time until fish is pliable but still icy. Let stand 10 minutes.
Steaks	50% (Med.)	4 to 7 min./lb.	Unwrap and place in baking dish or on roasting rack. Microwave for half of time. Separate and rearrange. Shield thin portions. Microwave remaining time until fish is pliable but icy in center. Let stand 5 to 10 minutes.
Lobster Tails, 2, about 8 oz. each	30% (Low)	10 to 14 min. total	Unwrap and place in baking dish or on roasting rack. Arrange with thickest portions toward outside. Shield thin portions after half of time. Microwave until tails are pliable but still icy in centers. Rearrange once or twice. Let stand 10 to 15 minutes.
4, about 8 oz. each	30% (Low)	15 to 19 min. total	
Oysters, Shucked, 1 pint	50% (Med.)	6 to 9 min./pint	Place plastic package in microwave oven. Microwave for half of time. Remove from package and place in baking dish. Microwave remaining time until oysters are pliable but still icy, stirring once. Let stand 10 minutes.
Scallops,	50% (Med.)	4½ to 6 min./lb.	Unwrap and place in baking dish. Microwave for half of time. Separate scallops as soon as possible. Microwave remaining time until cold but not icy, stirring 2 or 3 times. Rinse with cold water. Let stand 5 minutes.
Shrimp, Shelled, deveined	50% (Med.)	4 to 8 min./lb.	Unwrap and place in baking dish. Microwave for half of time. Separate shrimp as soon as possible. Microwave remaining time until cold but not icy, stirring 2 or 3 times. Rinse with cold water. Let stand 5 minutes.

Microwaving Fish & Shellfish

Type	Power Level	Time	Procedure
Fish, Whole, small	70% (Med. High)	6 to 9 min./lb.	Arrange in baking dish with backbones toward outside. Brush with melted butter or lemon juice. Cover with wax paper. Microwave for half of time. Rearrange. Microwave remaining time until fish flakes easily near thickest portion of backbone. Let stand, covered, 3 minutes.
Fillets	High	3½ to 6 min./lb.	Arrange in baking dish or on roasting rack. Brush with melted butter or lemon juice. Cover with wax paper. Microwave for half of time. Rearrange or rotate dish. Microwave remaining time until fish flakes easily with fork. Let stand, covered, 3 minutes.
Steaks	70% (Med. High)	7 to 9 min./lb.	Arrange in baking dish or on roasting rack. Brush with melted butter or lemon juice. Cover with wax paper. Microwave for half of time. Rearrange. Microwave remaining time until fish flakes easily with fork. Let stand, covered, 3 minutes.
Clams 1 lb., 12 to 15	High	3 to 5½ min./lb.	Scrub outside of shells thoroughly. Discard any broken or open clams. Soak in salted spring water for at least 3 hours to clean. Discard any open or floating clams. Rinse and drain clams. Place ½ cup water in 2-quart casserole. Microwave at High for 2 to 3½ minutes until boiling. Add clams. Cover. Microwave until clams open, stirring once.
Lobster Tails, 2, about 8 oz. each	50% (Med.)	7 to 11 min. total	Remove membrane from underside. Arrange in baking dish shell-side down. Brush with melted butter. Cover with plastic wrap. Microwave until lobster is firm and opaque, rotating dish once or twice. Shield 1 inch of flesh after half of time. Let stand, covered, 3 minutes.
4, about 8 oz. each	50% (Med.)	11 to 15 min. total	
Mussels, 1 lb., about 20	High	1½ to 3 min./lb.	Remove beard and scrub outside of shells thoroughly. Discard any broken or open mussels. Soak in salted spring water for at least 3 hours to clean. Discard any open or floating mussels. Rinse and drain mussels. Place ½ cup water in 2-quart casserole. Microwave at High for 2 to 3½ minutes until boiling. Add mussels. Cover. Microwave until mussels open, stirring once.
Scallops	70% (Med. High)	5 to 8 min./lb.	Arrange in single layer in baking dish. Cover with vented plastic wrap. Microwave for half of time. Stir to rearrange. Re-cover. Microwave remaining time until scallops are opaque. Let stand, covered, 1 to 2 minutes.
Shrimp	70% (Med. High)	5 to 8 min./lb.	Arrange in single layer in baking dish. Cover with vented plastic wrap. Microwave for half of time. Stir to rearrange. Re-cover. Microwave remaining time until shrimp are opaque. Let stand, covered, 1 to 2 minutes.

◄ Chicken Canapés

1 boneless chicken breast half
  (4 to 5 oz.) skin removed
¼ teaspoon dried tarragon
  leaves
2 slices onion, ¼ inch thick
2 tablespoons sliced almonds
1 tablespoon dairy sour cream
½ to 1 teaspoon Dijon mustard
¼ teaspoon salt
3 to 4 drops hot pepper sauce
2 zucchini, about 8 inches
  each
  Grated carrot (optional)

4 to 6 servings

Place chicken in 9-inch round baking dish. Sprinkle with tarragon. Top with onion. Cover with plastic wrap. Microwave at 70% (Medium High) for 2 to 5 minutes, or until chicken is no longer pink. Cool slightly. Chop onion slices. Place in small mixing bowl. Finely chop or shred chicken. Add to onion. Stir in remaining ingredients, except zucchini and carrot. Cut each zucchini crosswise into 6 equal pieces. Scoop out center of each zucchini piece with melon baller or small spoon to form a "cup." Fill each zucchini cup with chicken mixture. Garnish with grated carrot.

Breaded Chicken Strips

½ cup plain yogurt
1 tablespoon finely
  chopped onion
1 clove garlic, minced
¼ teaspoon fennel seed,
  crushed
1 boneless whole chicken
  breast (8 to 10 oz.) skin
  removed, cut into
  ½-inch strips
½ cup seasoned dry
  bread crumbs
2 tablespoons grated
  Parmesan cheese
¼ teaspoon paprika

14 to 16 appetizers

In 1-quart casserole, combine yogurt, onion, garlic and fennel. Add chicken strips. Cover. Chill for at least 2 hours. On wax paper, combine bread crumbs, Parmesan cheese and paprika. Roll each chicken strip in crumb mixture, pressing lightly to coat. Arrange strips on roasting rack. Microwave at 70% (Medium High) for 3½ to 5½ minutes, or until chicken is firm and no longer pink, rotating rack after half the time.

Oysters in Blankets

Marinade:
2 tablespoons white wine
2 teaspoons lemon juice
2 teaspoons olive oil
¼ teaspoon sugar
¼ teaspoon poultry seasoning
⅛ teaspoon hot pepper sauce
  Dash pepper

1 can (8 oz.) whole oysters,
  drained
2 slices boiled ham, cut into
  ½-inch strips
1 jar (5 oz.) cocktail onions

4 to 6 servings

In small mixing bowl, combine all marinade ingredients. Mix well. Gently stir in oysters to coat. Cover with plastic wrap. Marinate for 1 hour on counter.

Lift oysters from marinade. Wrap one ham strip around each oyster. Secure with wooden pick. Place one onion at end of each pick. Arrange on paper towel-lined plate. Microwave at 50% (Medium) for 2 to 4 minutes, or until hot, rotating plate once.

Sunny Turkey Roll-ups ▲

2 turkey cutlets (2 to 3 oz.
  each) ¼ inch thick

Marinade:
⅓ cup orange juice
2 teaspoons packed brown
  sugar
1 teaspoon vinegar
¼ teaspoon salt
¼ teaspoon ground ginger

Glaze:
2 tablespoons orange
  marmalade
1 teaspoon reserved marinade
½ teaspoon prepared mustard

6 frozen baby carrots, about
  1½ × 1 inch

4 servings

Cut turkey into 12 strips, about 3½ × ¾ inch. Set aside. In small
mixing bowl, combine all marinade ingredients. Mix well. Microwave
at High for 30 seconds to 1 minute, or until hot. Stir. Cool slightly.
Stir in turkey strips. Cover. Chill for 4 to 6 hours. Remove turkey
from marinade. Reserve 1 teaspoon marinade for glaze. In small
bowl, combine all glaze ingredients. Mix well.

Cut each carrot in half crosswise. Wrap each carrot piece with one
turkey strip. Secure with wooden pick. Dip in glaze. Arrange roll-ups
in circular pattern in 9-inch round baking dish. Microwave at High
for 2 to 4 minutes, or until turkey is no longer pink, rotating dish
once or twice.

Turkey Melon Bites ▲

¼ cup apricot jam
1 tablespoon teriyaki sauce
1 teaspoon honey
⅛ teaspoon salt
⅛ teaspoon ground cinnamon
⅛ teaspoon sesame oil
½ lb. turkey tenderloin, cut into
  1-inch cubes
14 to 16 cantaloupe or
  honeydew melon balls

14 to 16 appetizers

In small mixing bowl, blend all
ingredients, except turkey and
melon balls. Add turkey. Stir to
coat. Cover. Chill for at least
2 hours. To assemble, place
one turkey cube and one melon
ball on each wooden pick.
Arrange on roasting rack.
Microwave at 70% (Medium
High) for 3½ to 6 minutes, or
until turkey is firm and no longer
pink, rotating rack twice.

25

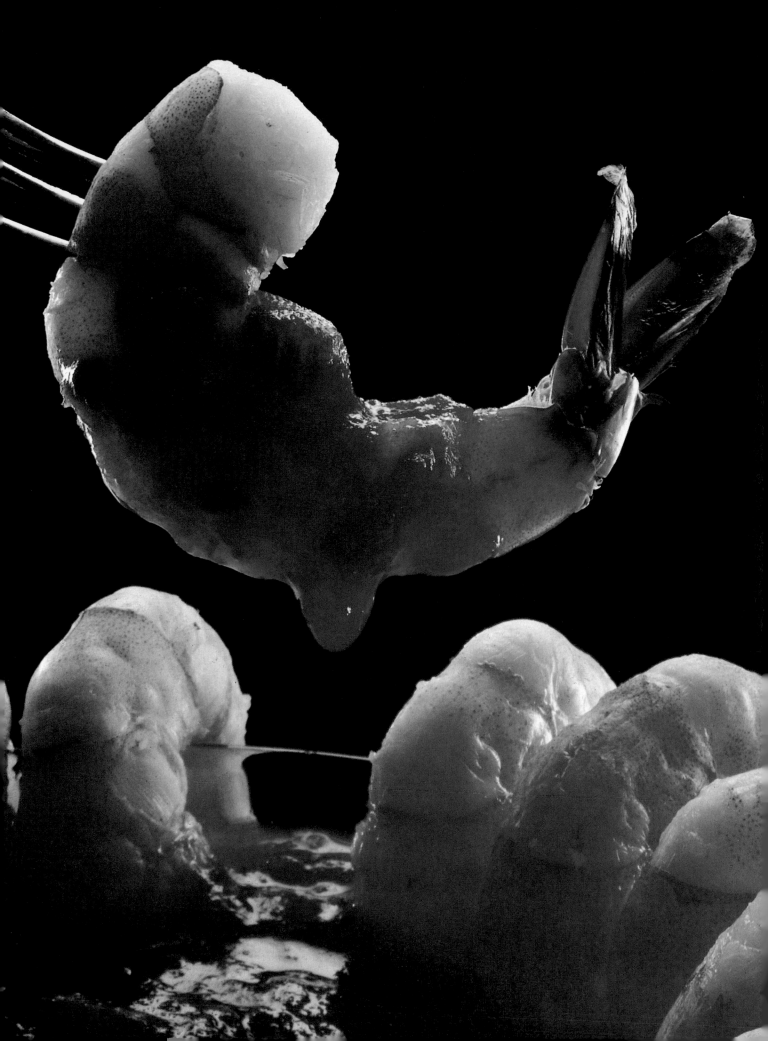

◄ Spiced Appetizer Shrimp

Marinade:

½ cup beer
1 small onion, sliced
1 tablespoon frozen grapefruit
   juice concentrate
1 teaspoon mixed pickling
   spices
⅛ teaspoon caraway seed
⅛ teaspoon cayenne
1 bay leaf

½ lb. extra-small shrimp,
   shelled and deveined
1 recipe Spicy Cocktail Sauce,
   page 148

4 servings

In 1-quart casserole, combine
all marinade ingredients.
Microwave at High for 1½ to
2½ minutes, or just until mixture
boils. Cool slightly. Stir in shrimp
to coat. Cover. Chill for 2 hours.
Prepare cocktail sauce as
directed. Chill. Lift shrimp from
marinade.

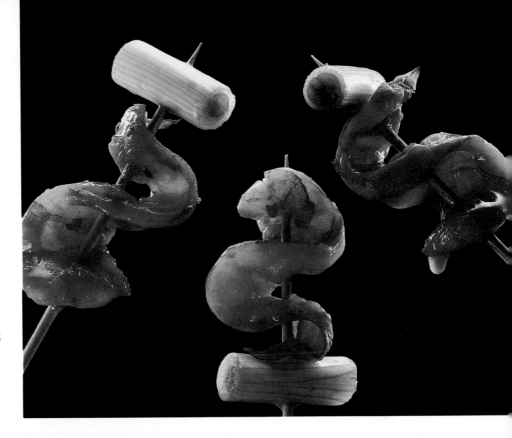

Arrange shrimp on roasting rack.
Cover with wax paper. Microwave at 70% (Medium High)
for 2½ to 4½ minutes, or until
shrimp are opaque, rearranging
once. Chill for at least 1 hour.
Arrange shrimp on crushed ice.
Serve with Spicy Cocktail Sauce.

Skewered Shrimp ▲

Marinade:

⅓ cup white wine
2 tablespoons soy sauce
1 tablespoon ketchup
1 teaspoon sugar
½ teaspoon sesame oil
¼ teaspoon dried crushed red
   pepper

1 lb. medium shrimp, shelled
   and deveined
6 to 7 green onions

4 to 6 servings

In small mixing bowl, combine
all marinade ingredients. Microwave at High for 1 minute, or
until very hot, but not boiling.
Stir. Cool slightly. Stir in shrimp
to coat. Cover. Chill for 3 to
4 hours. Drain. Cut shrimp in
half lengthwise. Thread each
half onto wooden pick. Cut
white part of green onions into
1-inch pieces. Place one onion
piece at end of each wooden
pick. Arrange on roasting rack.
Cover with wax paper. Microwave at 70% (Medium High) for
2 to 3½ minutes, or until shrimp
are opaque, rotating rack once.
Let stand for 1 minute.

Shrimp & Vegetable Ring

½ lb. small shrimp, shelled and
   deveined
3 cups fresh broccoli flowerets
3 cups fresh cauliflowerets
¼ cup water
1 recipe Tangy Dijon Butter,
   page 152

6 to 8 servings

Arrange shrimp in bottom of
9-inch ring dish. Set aside.

In 2-quart casserole, combine
broccoli, cauliflower and water.
Cover. Microwave at High for
6 to 7 minutes, or until vegetables are tender-crisp, stirring
once. Drain. Arrange vegetables
over shrimp, pressing firmly into
dish. Cover with vented plastic
wrap. Microwave at 50%
(Medium) for 7 to 10 minutes,
or until shrimp are opaque,
rotating dish twice. Let stand
while preparing Tangy Dijon
Butter. Invert dish onto serving
plate. Pour Tangy Dijon Butter
over top to serve.

Cocktail Meatballs in Chutney-Chili Sauce

Meatballs:
- 1 lb. ground turkey
- ¼ cup unseasoned dry bread crumbs
- 1 egg, beaten
- 1 tablespoon snipped fresh parsley
- ½ teaspoon salt
- ½ teaspoon chili powder
- ⅛ teaspoon pepper

Chutney-Chili Sauce:
- ½ cup chopped onion
- 1 tablespoon butter or margarine
- 1 clove garlic, minced
- 1½ teaspoons chili powder
- 1 can (8 oz.) tomato sauce
- ½ cup chutney

3 dozen appetizers

In medium mixing bowl, combine all meatball ingredients. Mix well. Shape into 36 meatballs, about 1¼ inches. Set aside.

In 2-quart casserole, combine onion, butter, garlic and chili powder. Cover. Microwave at High for 2½ to 3½ minutes, or until onion is tender. Add tomato sauce and chutney. Mix well. Add meatballs. Stir gently to coat meatballs with sauce. Re-cover. Reduce power to 70% (Medium High). Microwave for 8 to 13 minutes, or until meatballs are firm and cooked through, stirring gently after every 4 minutes.

Spicy Mexican Chicken Wings ▲

1½ lbs. chicken wings

Marinade:
- 1 small onion, minced
- 1 clove garlic, minced
- 3 tablespoons soy sauce
- 2 tablespoons water
- 2 tablespoons lime juice
- 1 tablespoon packed dark brown sugar
- 1 teaspoon ground coriander
- ½ teaspoon salt
- ½ teaspoon ground cumin
- ¼ teaspoon dried crushed red pepper
- ⅛ teaspoon pepper

4 to 6 servings

Separate each chicken wing into 3 parts at joints. Discard wing tips. In large plastic food storage bag, combine all marinade ingredients. Add chicken wings. Secure bag. Chill for at least 4 hours or overnight. Drain. Arrange chicken in 9-inch square baking dish. Cover with wax paper. Microwave at High for 7 to 11 minutes, or until chicken is no longer pink, rearranging chicken once or twice.

Greek Meatballs

Meatballs:
- 1 lb. ground turkey
- ¼ cup finely chopped onion
- 1 egg, beaten
- 2 tablespoons unseasoned dry bread crumbs
- 2 tablespoons chopped black olives
- 2 tablespoons snipped fresh parsley
- 1 clove garlic, minced
- 1 teaspoon dried oregano leaves
- ¾ teaspoon salt
- ¼ teaspoon ground cinnamon
- ⅛ teaspoon ground allspice
- ⅛ teaspoon pepper

Sauce:
- 1 can (8 oz.) tomato sauce
- 1 tablespoon snipped fresh parsley
- ½ teaspoon sugar
- ¼ teaspoon salt
  Dash pepper

3 dozen appetizers

How to Microwave Greek Meatballs

Combine all meatball ingredients in medium mixing bowl. Mix well. Shape into 36 meatballs, about 1¼ inches. Place in 10-inch square casserole. Set aside.

Blend all sauce ingredients in 2-cup measure. Pour over meatballs. Cover with wax paper.

Microwave at 70% (Medium High) for 8 to 13 minutes, or until meatballs are firm and cooked through, stirring gently after every 4 minutes.

Seafood-stuffed Brie

1 wheel (8 oz.) Brie cheese,
    4½ × 1¼ inches
2 tablespoons chopped
    pecans
1 tablespoon butter or
    margarine
1 can (4¼ oz.) small shrimp,
    rinsed and drained
½ cup finely shredded
    Colby cheese

       6 to 8 servings

Cut Brie in half crosswise. Place bottom half, cut-side-up on serving plate. Trim and discard crust from top of remaining half. Set aside. In small bowl, combine pecans and butter. Microwave at High for 2½ to 3 minutes, or until pecans are toasted, stirring after every minute. In small mixing bowl, mash shrimp with fork. Stir in pecans and Colby cheese. Press half of shrimp mixture onto bottom half of Brie. Cover with top half of Brie. Press remaining shrimp mixture onto Brie. Microwave at 50% (Medium) for 2 to 2½ minutes, or until Brie is warm and softened, rotating plate after every minute. Serve with assorted crackers.

Fresh Seafood Sampler with Orange Curry Butter

½ cup butter or margarine
1 tablespoon snipped
   fresh parsley
½ teaspoon grated
   orange peel
¼ teaspoon curry powder
⅛ teaspoon cayenne
2 cups fresh broccoli flowerets
12 oz. fresh baby carrots,
   2-inch
½ lb. fresh mussels
½ lb. fresh medium shrimp,
   shelled and deveined
   Lemon wedges

6 to 8 servings

In 4-cup measure, combine butter, parsley, orange peel, curry powder, and cayenne. Microwave at High for 1½ to 2½ minutes, or until butter melts and mixture begins to boil. Set aside.

Arrange broccoli in center of large platter. Arrange half of carrots on either side of broccoli. Drizzle vegetables with 2 tablespoons of butter mixture. Cover with plastic wrap. Microwave at High for 4 minutes, rotating platter after half the time. Arrange mussels and shrimp on either side of carrots. Drizzle with 2 tablespoons of butter mixture. Re-cover. Reduce power to 50% (Medium). Microwave for 6 to 9 minutes, or until mussels open and shrimp are opaque, rotating platter twice. Serve with remaining butter mixture and lemon wedges.

Cinnamon & Spice Chicken Wings ▲

1 lb. chicken wings
1 can (8 oz.) pineapple
   chunks, undrained
1 cup chopped apple
1 medium green pepper,
   cut into 1-inch chunks
¼ cup packed dark
   brown sugar

2 tablespoons raisins
1 tablespoon cornstarch
½ teaspoon salt
½ teaspoon curry powder
¼ teaspoon ground cinnamon
⅛ teaspoon cayenne

6 servings

Separate each chicken wing into 3 parts at joints. Discard wing tips. In large plastic food storage bag, combine remaining ingredients. Add chicken wings. Secure bag. Chill overnight, turning bag over once or twice. Pour chicken and marinade into 2-quart casserole. Cover. Microwave at High for 11 to 13 minutes, or until chicken is no longer pink and green pepper is tender, stirring 2 or 3 times.

Scallop-stuffed Mushrooms ▲

⅓ cup sherry
1 teaspoon olive oil
2 tablespoons sliced
   green onion
1 clove garlic, minced
¼ teaspoon dried thyme leaves
1 tablespoon butter or
   margarine

⅓ cup seasoned dry bread
   crumbs
1 tablespoon snipped fresh
   parsley
36 bay scallops, (about ½ lb.)
36 fresh mushrooms (about
   1 lb.) stems removed

3 dozen appetizers

In small mixing bowl, combine sherry, olive oil, onion, garlic and thyme. Cover. Microwave at High for 1½ to 2 minutes, or until mixture boils. Cool slightly. Place butter in small bowl. Microwave at High for 30 to 45 seconds, or until butter melts. Stir in bread crumbs and parsley. Cover. Set aside. Add scallops to sherry mixture. Toss to coat. Cover. Chill for 1 to 2 hours. Drain. Place one scallop in center of each mushroom cap. Sprinkle with bread crumb mixture, pressing lightly. Arrange half of stuffed mushrooms on paper towel-lined plate. Cover with paper towel. Microwave at 50% (Medium) for 2½ to 5 minutes, or until scallops are firm and opaque, rotating plate after every minute. Repeat with remaining stuffed mushrooms.

Shrimp & Chicken Kebabs

Shrimp Marinade:
3 tablespoons olive oil
1 tablespoon orange juice
1 clove garlic, minced

6 extra-large shrimp, shelled
   and deveined

Chicken Marinade:
3 tablespoons soy sauce
2 tablespoons packed brown
   sugar
2 tablespoons orange juice
½ teaspoon paprika
1 clove garlic, minced

3 chicken wings
6 small orange wedges
6 green onions, about 3 inches
   each*
6 wooden skewers, 6-inch

6 servings

In small mixing bowl, blend all Shrimp Marinade ingredients. Add shrimp. Stir to coat. Cover. Set aside. In small mixing bowl, blend all Chicken Marinade ingredients. Microwave at High for 1 to 2 minutes, or until hot. Cool slightly. Separate each chicken wing into 3 parts at joints. Discard wing tips. Add chicken to marinade. Stir to coat. Cover. Chill shrimp and chicken for at least 4 hours, stirring occasionally.

For each kebab, assemble orange wedge, chicken, onion and shrimp on wooden skewer. Repeat to make 6 kebabs. Arrange on roasting rack. Cover with wax paper. Microwave at 70% (Medium High) for 5½ to 9 minutes, or until shrimp are opaque and chicken is no longer pink, turning kebabs over and rotating rack once.

*Cut several slashes in green end of each onion. Soak in ice water until curled.

Pepperoni-stuffed ▲ Scallops

12 sea scallops (about ½ lb.) 1½ inches
6 thin slices pepperoni, cut in half
6 garlic Melba cracker rounds, finely crushed
1½ teaspoons grated Parmesan cheese
¼ teaspoon dried parsley flakes
Dash pepper

4 servings

Cut a lengthwise slit in center of each scallop, but do not cut completely through. Stuff each scallop with pepperoni half. Arrange scallops in circular pattern on paper towel-lined plate. Set aside.

In custard cup, combine cracker crumbs, Parmesan cheese, parsley and pepper. Sprinkle each scallop with ½ teaspoon of crumb mixture. Microwave at 70% (Medium High) for 2 to 4 minutes, or until scallops are firm and opaque, rotating plate once. Serve hot.

Clam-stuffed Mushrooms

3 slices bacon, cut-up
8 oz. fresh mushrooms, stems removed and reserved
2 tablespoons finely chopped onion
⅛ teaspoon dried marjoram leaves
⅛ teaspoon salt
Dash crushed sage leaves
Dash pepper
3 tablespoons seasoned dry bread crumbs
1 tablespoon snipped fresh parsley
1 can (6½ oz.) minced clams, drained

4 servings

Place bacon in small mixing bowl. Microwave at High for 2½ to 3½ minutes, or until crisp, stirring once. Drain, reserving 1 tablespoon bacon fat. In small mixing bowl, combine reserved bacon fat, ⅓ cup chopped mushroom stems, onion, marjoram, salt, sage and pepper. Mix well. Microwave at High for 1½ to 2¼ minutes, or until onion is tender-crisp, stirring once. Stir in bacon, bread crumbs, parsley and clams. Fill mushroom caps. Arrange on paper towel-lined plate. Microwave at High for 1½ to 3 minutes, or until hot, rotating plate once.

Spiced Turkey-stuffed Chilies

1 can (7 oz.) whole green chilies
¼ lb. ground turkey
¼ teaspoon ground cumin
⅛ teaspoon garlic powder
⅛ teaspoon salt
⅛ teaspoon ground oregano
⅛ teaspoon ground cinnamon
1 jar (8 oz.) pasteurized process cheese spread

14 to 18 appetizers

Drain chilies on paper towels. Slice each chili crosswise into about 1-inch pieces. Set aside. In small mixing bowl, combine turkey, cumin, garlic powder, salt, oregano and cinnamon. Mix well. Spoon small amount of turkey mixture onto center of each pepper piece. Set aside. Spoon cheese into bottom of 9-inch round baking dish. Microwave at 50% (Medium) for 2 to 3 minutes, or until cheese can be stirred smooth. Arrange pepper pieces on cheese. Cover with wax paper. Increase power to 70% (Medium High). Microwave for 4 to 6 minutes, or until turkey is firm, rotating dish after half the time.

33

Clams Royale

12 to 15 small hard-shell
    clams (about 1 lb.)
½ cup water
3 tablespoons butter or
    margarine
1 tablespoon snipped
    fresh parsley
2 teaspoons lemon juice
¼ teaspoon paprika
⅛ teaspoon dried
    thyme leaves
⅛ teaspoon pepper
¼ cup finely chopped fully
    cooked ham
¼ cup unseasoned dry
    bread crumbs

4 to 6 servings

Scrub outside of clam shells
thoroughly, discarding any
broken or open clams. Soak
clams in salted water for at least
3 hours to clean. Rinse and
drain clams. Place water in
2-quart casserole. Microwave
at High for 2 to 3½ minutes, or
until water boils. Add clams.
Cover. Microwave at High for
3 to 5½ minutes, or until clams
open, stirring once. Remove
clams from casserole as they
begin to open. Remove each
clam from shell. Reserve half
of each shell. Mince clams.
Set aside.

In small mixing bowl, combine
butter, parsley, lemon juice,
paprika, thyme and pepper.
Microwave at High for 1 to
1½ minutes, or until butter melts
and mixture is hot. Stir in ham,
bread crumbs and minced
clams. Spoon into reserved
shells. Arrange shells on plate.
Microwave at 50% (Medium)
for 3 to 4 minutes, or until hot.

Salmon Cocktail Toasts

⅓ cup chopped fresh
    mushrooms
2 tablespoons chopped
    green pepper
2 tablespoons chopped onion
1 can (7½ oz.) salmon,
    drained and flaked
½ cup peeled shredded
    cucumber
½ cup ricotta cheese
¼ cup grated Parmesan
    cheese
½ teaspoon Worcestershire
    sauce
¼ teaspoon dried dill weed
¼ teaspoon seasoned salt
⅛ teaspoon pepper
24 slices cocktail bread, toasted
24 thin slices cucumber, cut in
    half (optional)

10 to 12 servings

In 1-quart casserole, combine mushrooms, green pepper and onion. Cover. Microwave at High for 2 to 3 minutes, or until mushrooms are tender, stirring once. Remove bones and skin from salmon. Add salmon, shredded cucumber, ricotta and Parmesan cheeses, Worcestershire sauce, dill weed, seasoned salt and pepper to mushroom mixture. Mix well. Spread about 1 tablespoon salmon mixture on each slice of bread. Cut each slice in half diagonally. Arrange 24 halves on paper towel-lined plate. Microwave at 50% (Medium) for 3 to 5 minutes, or until hot, rearranging slices once. Top each half with cucumber slice. Repeat with remaining toasts. Serve hot.

Appetizer Crab Quiches ▲

1 can (6 oz.) crab meat,
    rinsed, drained and
    cartilage removed
½ cup shredded carrot
½ cup finely shredded
    Monterey Jack cheese
2 tablespoons sliced green
    onion
1 teaspoon all-purpose flour

¼ teaspoon ground nutmeg
¼ teaspoon salt
⅛ teaspoon pepper
4 scallop shells or ramekins,
    4-inch
¼ cup half-and-half
1 egg
    Paprika

4 servings

In small mixing bowl, combine crab meat, carrot, cheese, onion, flour, nutmeg, salt and pepper. Spoon one-fourth of mixture into each scallop shell. Arrange shells on serving platter. Set aside.

In 1-cup measure, beat half-and-half and egg. Pour about 2 tablespoons egg mixture over each filled shell. Sprinkle with paprika. Cover with wax paper. Microwave at 50% (Medium) for 8 to 10½ minutes, or until mixture is firm in center, rotating shells after every 2 minutes. Let stand, covered, for 5 minutes.

Steamed Stuffed Wontons

1½ teaspoons butter or
　　　margarine
　1 tablespoon sesame seed
　1 egg
　1 tablespoon milk

Filling:
　¾ cup cooked shredded
　　　chicken
　¼ cup grated carrot
　2 teaspoons finely chopped
　　　green onion
　1 tablespoon soy sauce
　¼ teaspoon sesame oil
　⅛ teaspoon ground ginger

12 to 15 wonton skins,
　　　4-inch squares
2½ cups water
　2 teaspoons soy sauce
　1 teaspoon instant chicken
　　　bouillon granules
　5 to 6 drops hot pepper
　　　sauce

12 to 15 appetizers

How to Microwave Steamed Stuffed Wontons

Place butter in 1-cup measure. Microwave at High for 30 to 45 seconds, or until butter melts.

Stir in sesame seed. Microwave at High for 2½ to 4½ minutes, or until light golden brown, stirring after every minute. Let stand for 2 to 3 minutes. Drain on paper towel. Set aside.

Beat egg and milk in small bowl. Set aside. In small mixing bowl, combine all filling ingredients. Mix well. Set aside. Brush edges of each wonton skin with egg-milk mixture.

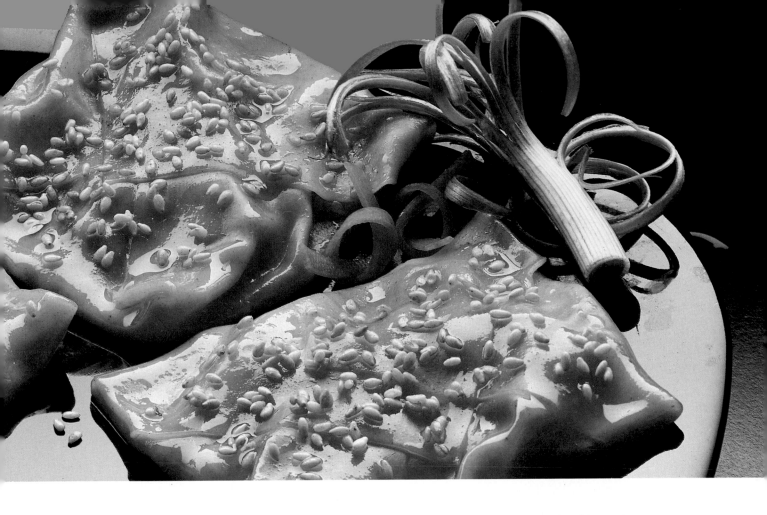

Spoon 2 teaspoons filling diagonally across center of each wonton skin. Fold one corner over filling. Fold in sides and then remaining corner. Repeat with remaining wonton skins.

Combine water, soy sauce, bouillon and hot pepper sauce in 10-inch square casserole. Cover. Microwave at High for 10 to 11 minutes, or until mixture boils. Add prepared wontons. Re-cover.

Shake casserole slightly to coat wontons with liquid. Microwave at High for 3½ to 5½ minutes, or until tender and translucent. Remove with slotted spoon to serving dish. Sprinkle with toasted sesame seed.

Six-layer Taco Dip

2 cups shredded zucchini
1 cup cut-up cooked chicken
   or turkey
⅛ teaspoon salt
   Dash pepper
½ cup chopped green pepper
2 tablespoons sliced green
   onion
⅔ cup taco sauce
1 cup shredded Monterey
   Jack cheese

About 3 cups

Place zucchini in shallow 1-quart casserole. Cover. Microwave at High for 3 to 4 minutes, or until tender, stirring once. Let stand, covered, for 5 minutes. Drain thoroughly, pressing to remove excess moisture.

In same casserole, spread zucchini evenly over bottom of casserole. Spread chicken over zucchini. Sprinkle with salt and pepper. Add layer of green pepper and onion. Pour taco sauce over layers. Cover. Microwave at High for 4 to 7 minutes, or until hot and bubbly around edges. Sprinkle evenly with Monterey Jack cheese. Reduce power to 50% (Medium). Microwave for 2 to 3 minutes, or until cheese melts, rotating casserole after every minute. Serve with tortilla chips.

Hot Shrimp Dip ▲

⅓ cup chopped celery
2 tablespoons sliced
   green onion
1 clove garlic, minced
1 tablespoon butter or
   margarine
½ teaspoon ground cumin
1 pkg. (3 oz.) cream cheese

½ cup plain yogurt
1 tablespoon ketchup
1 can (4¼ oz.) medium shrimp,
   rinsed and drained
4 seafood sticks (about ¼ lb.)
   chopped
½ cup shredded Cheddar
   cheese

2 cups

In 1-quart casserole or soufflé dish, combine celery, onion, garlic, butter and cumin. Cover. Microwave at High for 2 to 3 minutes, or until vegetables are tender. Set aside. Place cream cheese in small mixing bowl. Microwave at 50% (Medium) for 30 to 45 seconds, or until softened. Stir into vegetable mixture. Blend in yogurt and ketchup. Add shrimp and seafood sticks. Mix well. Sprinkle with Cheddar cheese. Microwave at 50% (Medium) for 4 to 5 minutes, or until cheese melts and dip is hot. Let stand for 5 minutes. Serve with bread sticks.

Spinach Chicken Dip

1 boneless chicken breast half
    (4 to 5 oz.) skin removed
1 pkg. (10 oz.) frozen chopped
    spinach
2 tablespoons chopped onion
1 pkg. (3 oz.) cream cheese
½ cup shredded Swiss cheese
¼ cup mayonnaise
¼ cup sliced black olives
¼ cup milk
½ teaspoon salt
⅛ teaspoon ground nutmeg
⅛ teaspoon fennel seed,
    crushed
⅛ teaspoon pepper

About 1½ cups

Place chicken in 9-inch round baking dish. Cover with wax paper. Microwave at 70% (Medium High) for 2 to 5 minutes, or until chicken is no longer pink. Set aside.

Unwrap spinach and place on plate. Microwave at High for 4 to 5½ minutes, or until warm. Drain thoroughly, pressing to remove excess moisture. Set aside.

Place onion in 1-quart casserole. Microwave at High for 45 seconds to 1 minute, or until tender-crisp. Stir in cream cheese. Finely chop or shred chicken. Add chicken, spinach and remaining ingredients to cream cheese mixture. Mix well. Reduce power to 70% (Medium High). Microwave for 2½ to 4 minutes, or until heated through and cheese melts, stirring once. Serve warm with crackers or chips.

Chicken & Artichoke Dip

1 boneless chicken breast half
   (4 to 5 oz.) skin removed,
   cut into ½-inch cubes
1 jar (6 oz.) marinated
   artichoke hearts, drained
   (reserve marinade)
3 tablespoons sliced green
   onions, divided
¼ teaspoon salt
⅛ teaspoon pepper
½ cup shredded Cheddar
   cheese
⅓ cup mayonnaise
2 tablespoons plain yogurt

About 1½ cups

How to Microwave Chicken & Artichoke Dip

Place chicken in small mixing bowl. Add reserved marinade from artichokes. Cover. Chill for at least 1 hour.

Chop artichoke hearts. Set aside. Drain chicken. Add 1 tablespoon onion. Re-cover.

Microwave at High for 1½ to 2½ minutes, or until chicken is no longer pink, stirring after every minute. Drain.

40

Smoked Oyster Dip

- 2 tablespoons finely chopped celery
- 1 tablespoon finely chopped onion
- 2 teaspoons butter or margarine
- 1 can (3.66 oz.) smoked oysters, drained and coarsely chopped
- ⅓ cup dairy sour cream
- ¼ cup plain yogurt
- 2 tablespoons mayonnaise
- 1 tablespoon snipped fresh parsley
- 2 teaspoons lemon juice
- ¼ teaspoon freshly ground pepper

About 1 cup

In small mixing bowl, combine celery, onion and butter. Cover with plastic wrap. Microwave at High for 1 to 2½ minutes, or until tender-crisp. Stir in remaining ingredients. Chill for at least 1 hour. Serve with assorted raw vegetables.

Stir in artichokes, salt and pepper. Spread mixture over bottom of shallow 1-quart casserole. Set aside.

Combine Cheddar cheese, mayonnaise and yogurt in small mixing bowl. Mix well. Spread evenly over chicken and artichoke mixture.

Sprinkle with remaining 2 tablespoons onion. Cover. Microwave at 50% (Medium) for 2 to 4 minutes, or until heated through. Serve warm with assorted crackers.

Easy Chicken Pâté

1 lb. chicken livers, rinsed
   and drained
⅓ cup chopped fresh
   mushrooms
¼ cup butter or margarine,
   cut-up
3 tablespoons chopped onion
2 tablespoons finely chopped
   celery
2 tablespoons dry vermouth
1 tablespoon snipped
   fresh parsley
1 teaspoon instant chicken
   bouillon granules
½ teaspoon salt
¼ teaspoon dried rosemary
   leaves
⅛ teaspoon dried thyme leaves
⅛ teaspoon ground mace
⅛ teaspoon pepper
   Dash garlic powder
   Snipped fresh parsley
   (optional)

2 cups

Butter a 2-cup crock or serving
dish. Set aside. In 1½-quart
casserole, combine all ingredients, except parsley. Cover. Microwave at 70% (Medium High)
for 11 to 15 minutes, or until
chicken livers are no longer pink,
stirring after every 5 minutes.

In food processor or blender
container, combine chicken
mixture and cooking liquid.
Process until mixture is smooth.
Pour into prepared crock.
Cover. Chill for at least 6 hours
or overnight. Garnish with
parsley. Serve with toasted
French bread slices.

Chicken Mousse with Seafood

2 chicken thighs (about 3 oz. each) skin removed
2 teaspoons chopped onion
2 teaspoons all-purpose flour
¼ teaspoon Worcestershire sauce
⅛ teaspoon dried basil leaves
⅛ teaspoon salt
Dash ground nutmeg
Dash pepper
¾ cup half-and-half
3 mock crab legs (about 3 oz.) cut-up
Shredded zucchini or snipped fresh parsley (optional)

8 to 10 servings

Remove chicken from bones. Set aside.

In food processor or blender container, combine chicken, onion, flour, Worcestershire sauce, basil, salt, nutmeg and pepper. Process until finely chopped. With machine running, add half-and-half. Process until mixture is smooth, stopping to scrape side of container if necessary.

Arrange mock crab pieces in bottom of 15-oz. round individual casserole. Pour chicken mixture evenly over mock crab. Cover with wax paper. Microwave at 50% (Medium) for 5 to 12 minutes, or until center is soft set, rotating dish once. Chill for at least 3 hours. Invert onto serving plate. Garnish with zucchini or parsley. Serve with crackers.

Soups & Stews

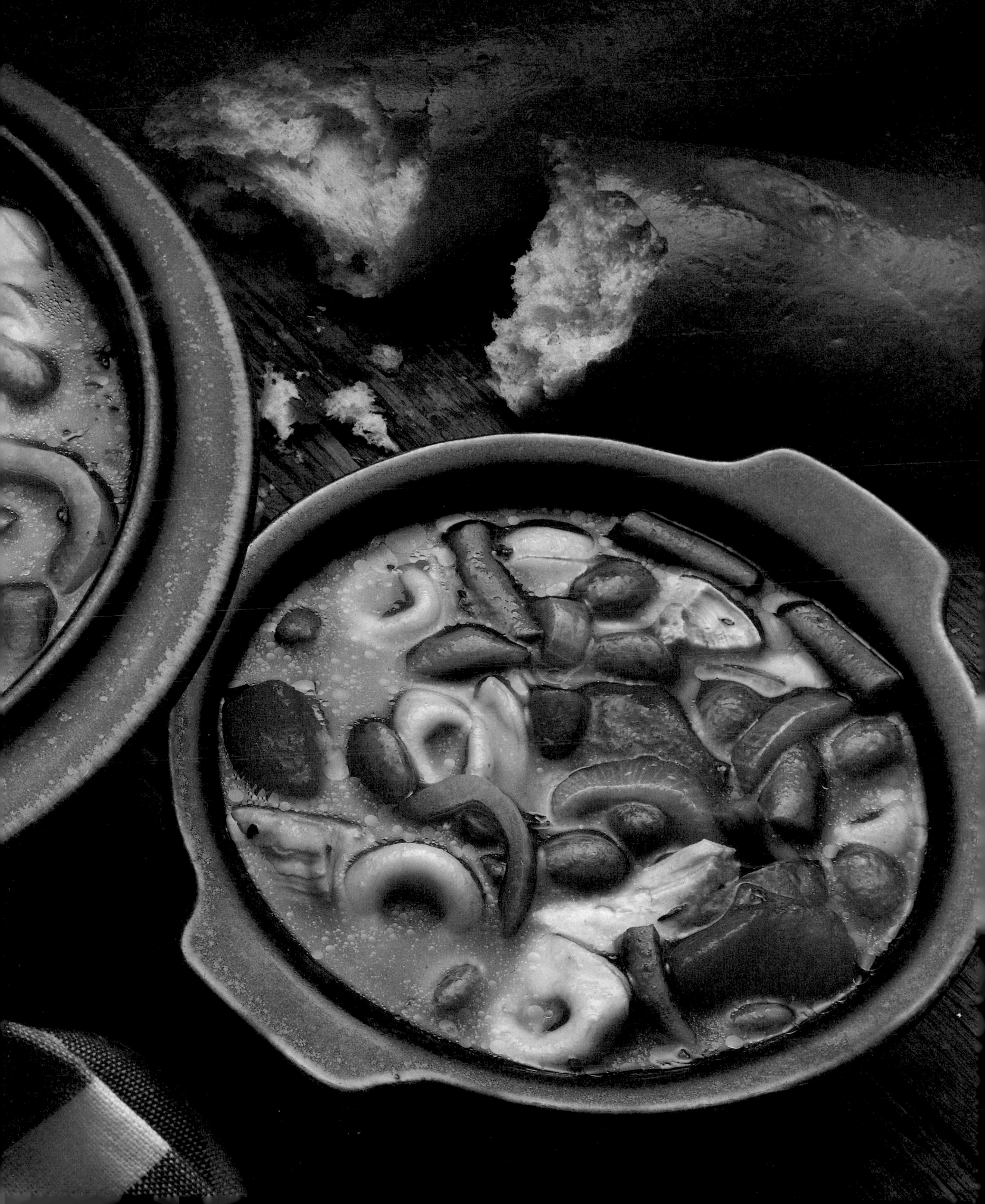

Savory Chicken & Rice Soup

- 3 tablespoons butter or margarine
- ⅓ cup chopped carrot
- ⅓ cup chopped celery
- 2 tablespoons sliced green onion
- 1 tablespoon snipped fresh parsley
- 1 clove garlic, minced
- 1 teaspoon dried summer savory leaves
- ⅛ teaspoon pepper
- 3 tablespoons all-purpose flour
- 1 cup sliced fresh mushrooms
- 1 cup cooked brown rice
- 1 boneless whole chicken breast (8 to 10 oz.) skin removed, cut into 1 × ¼-inch strips
- 1 can (14½ oz.) ready-to-serve chicken broth
- ¼ cup white wine
- ½ teaspoon salt
- 1 cup milk
- 2 egg yolks

4 to 6 servings

In 3-quart casserole, combine butter, carrot, celery, onion, parsley, garlic, summer savory and pepper. Cover. Microwave at High for 6 to 7 minutes, or until vegetables are tender, stirring once or twice. Stir in flour, mushrooms and brown rice. Stir in chicken, broth, wine and salt. Re-cover. Microwave at High for 8 to 10 minutes, or until mixture thickens and mushrooms are tender, stirring after every 3 minutes. Set aside. In small mixing bowl, blend milk and egg yolks. Pour slowly into broth mixture, stirring until blended. Re-cover. Reduce power to 50% (Medium). Microwave for 3 to 7 minutes, or until chicken is no longer pink and soup is heated through, stirring after half the time.

Chicken-Cheddar Soup ▶

2½ to 3-lb. broiler-fryer
      chicken, cut into 8 pieces
  1 clove garlic, cut into
      4 pieces
  ½ teaspoon dried oregano
      leaves
  ¼ teaspoon celery salt
  ¼ teaspoon whole cumin
      seed
  ½ cup water
  1 tablespoon butter or
      margarine
  ⅓ cup chopped onion
  ½ teaspoon ground cumin
  1 can (16 oz.) whole
      tomatoes, cut-up
  2 tablespoons canned
      chopped green chilies
  2 tablespoons all-purpose
      flour
  2 cups finely shredded mild
      Cheddar cheese
  ½ teaspoon salt
  ⅛ teaspoon cayenne
  1 cup half-and-half

4 to 6 servings

Arrange chicken in deep
3-quart casserole with thickest
portions toward outside of
casserole. Add garlic, oregano,
celery salt, cumin seed and
water. Cover. Microwave at High
for 16 to 20 minutes, or until
chicken near bone is no longer
pink, turning chicken over once.
Skim fat. Strain and reserve
broth. Set aside. Remove
chicken from bones. Cut into
bite-size pieces. Set aside.

In same casserole, combine
butter, onion and ground cumin.
Cover. Microwave at High for
3 to 6 minutes, or until onion is
tender. Add reserved broth,
chicken, tomatoes and chilies.
Mix well. In large plastic food
storage bag, shake flour and
cheese until cheese is coated.
Stir into chicken and tomato
mixture. Blend in remaining
ingredients. Re-cover. Reduce
power to 50% (Medium). Microwave for 15 to 20 minutes, or
until heated through and
cheese melts, stirring after
every 5 minutes.

Minestrone-Chicken Stew

  2 tablespoons olive oil
  1 medium onion, cut in half
      lengthwise and thinly sliced
  1 teaspoon celery salt
  ½ teaspoon dried marjoram
      leaves
  ¼ teaspoon garlic powder
  ¼ teaspoon dried rosemary
      leaves
  ⅛ teaspoon dried thyme
      leaves
  2 medium tomatoes, peeled,
      seeded and cut into 1-inch
      pieces

  1 can (16 oz.) pinto beans,
      rinsed and drained
  1 pkg. (9 oz.) frozen cut
      green beans
  1 pkg. (/ oz.) uncooked
      cheese-filled tortellini
  1⅓ cups water
  1½ cups vegetable juice
      cocktail
  1 can (10¾ oz.) condensed
      chicken broth
  1 cup cut-up cooked chicken

6 to 8 servings

In deep 3-quart casserole, combine olive oil, onion, celery salt,
marjoram, garlic powder, rosemary and thyme. Cover. Microwave at
High for 4 to 6 minutes, or until onion is tender, stirring after every
2 minutes. Stir in remaining ingredients, except chicken. Re-cover.
Microwave at High for 20 to 25 minutes, or until tortellini is tender,
stirring after every 10 minutes. Stir in chicken. Re-cover. Microwave
at High for 5 minutes, or until heated through.

47

Chicken-Okra Gumbo

2½ to 3-lb. broiler-fryer
     chicken, cut into 8 pieces
 ½ teaspoon dried thyme
     leaves
 ¼ teaspoon dried basil leaves
 ⅛ teaspoon cayenne
 1 clove garlic, minced
 1 bay leaf
 1 cup water
 2 tablespoons vegetable oil
 1 medium onion, thinly sliced
 1 medium green pepper,
     chopped
 3 tablespoons all-purpose
     flour
 1 can (16 oz.) whole
     tomatoes, cut-up
 1 pkg. (10 oz.) frozen cut
     okra
 1 cup cubed fully cooked
     ham, ½-inch cubes
 ¾ cup vegetable juice
     cocktail
 1 teaspoon salt
 1 teaspoon Worcestershire
     sauce
 ¼ teaspoon hot pepper sauce

6 to 8 servings

How to Microwave Chicken-Okra Gumbo

Arrange chicken in 3-quart casserole with thickest portions toward outside of casserole. Sprinkle with thyme, basil and cayenne. Add garlic, bay leaf and water. Cover.

Microwave at High for 16 to 20 minutes, or until chicken near bone is no longer pink, turning chicken over once. Skim fat. Strain and reserve broth. Set aside.

Remove chicken from bones. Cut into bite-size pieces. Set aside.

48

Combine oil, onion and green pepper in same casserole. Cover. Microwave at High for 5 to 7 minutes, or until tender, stirring once.

Stir in flour. Add remaining ingredients, reserved broth and chicken. Re-cover.

Microwave at High for 20 to 25 minutes, or until mixture thickens and flavors are blended, stirring 3 times. Serve over hot cooked rice.

Lemony Chicken & Rice Soup

3 tablespoons butter or margarine, divided
⅓ cup sliced almonds
1 cup shredded carrots
2 tablespoons sliced green onion
1 tablespoon snipped fresh parsley
2 tablespoons all-purpose flour
2 cans (14½ oz. each) ready-to-serve chicken broth
3 tablespoons fresh lemon juice
½ teaspoon salt
⅛ teaspoon white pepper
3 egg yolks, beaten
1 cup cut-up cooked chicken
1 cup cooked rice

4 to 6 servings

In 1-quart casserole combine 1 tablespoon butter and almonds. Microwave at High for 3½ to 4½ minutes, or just until almonds begin to brown, stirring once. Set aside. In 2-quart casserole, combine carrots, onion and parsley with remaining 2 tablespoons butter. Cover. Microwave at High for 3 to 4 minutes, or until carrots are tender-crisp, stirring once. Stir in flour. Blend in broth, lemon juice, salt and pepper. Microwave, uncovered, at High for 10 to 16 minutes, or until mixture boils. Whisk small amount of hot broth mixture into egg yolks. Return egg yolk mixture to hot broth, blending with whisk. Stir in chicken and rice. Reduce power to 50% (Medium). Microwave for 3 to 6 minutes, or until mixture is slightly thickened and chicken is heated through, stirring twice. Stir in almonds.

Chicken & Succotash Stew

2 tablespoons butter or margarine
1 cup uncooked broken spaghetti
1 clove garlic, minced
2½ to 3-lb. broiler-fryer chicken, cut into 8 pieces, skin removed
1 can (15 oz.) garbanzo beans, drained
1 pkg. (10 oz.) frozen mixed vegetables
1⅓ cups water
1 can (10½ oz.) condensed chicken and rice soup
½ teaspoon salt
½ teaspoon bouquet garni seasoning
⅛ teaspoon pepper

6 to 8 servings

In 3-quart casserole, combine butter, spaghetti and garlic. Microwave at High for 2½ to 3½ minutes, or until spaghetti is golden brown, stirring after every minute. Add chicken and remaining ingredients. Stir. Cover. Microwave at High for 20 to 25 minutes, or until chicken near bone is no longer pink and spaghetti is tender, stirring and turning chicken over after every 5 minutes.

Tomato-Tortilla Soup ▶

- 2 corn tortillas, 6-inch
  Vegetable oil
- 1 tablespoon vegetable oil
- ½ cup chopped celery
- ⅓ cup chopped onion
- 2 tablespoons snipped fresh parsley
- ¾ teaspoon ground cumin
- ¼ teaspoon garlic powder
- ¼ teaspoon ground coriander
- 1 can (28 oz.) whole tomatoes, cut-up
- 1 cup cooked white rice
- 1 cup julienne cooked chicken breast (2 × ¼-inch strips)
- 1 cup ready-to-serve chicken broth
- 2 tablespoons canned chopped green chilies
- 2 teaspoons sugar
- ½ teaspoon salt
- ½ cup finely shredded Cheddar cheese

4 to 5 servings

Cut tortillas into ¼-inch strips. In small skillet, fry tortilla strips in ¼ inch hot oil until golden brown and crisp. Drain on paper towels. Set aside. In 2-quart casserole, combine 1 tablespoon oil, celery, onion, parsley, cumin, garlic powder and coriander. Cover. Microwave at High for 3½ to 4½ minutes, or until vegetables are tender. Stir in remaining ingredients, except tortilla strips and cheese. Re-cover. Microwave at High for 8 to 10 minutes, or until hot, stirring twice. Sprinkle with tortilla strips and cheese.

Chicken-Spinach Soup

- 2½ to 3-lb. broiler-fryer chicken, cut into 8 pieces
- 1 stalk celery, cut into 4 pieces
- 1 carrot, cut into 4 pieces
- 1 onion, cut into 4 pieces
- ½ teaspoon dried thyme leaves
- ¼ cup water
- 1 pkg. (10 oz.) frozen chopped spinach
- 2 tablespoons butter or margarine

- 2 tablespoons all-purpose flour
- ¾ teaspoon salt
- ¼ teaspoon pepper
- ¼ teaspoon ground nutmeg
- ⅛ teaspoon dried thyme leaves
- 2½ cups milk
- ¼ cup chopped water chestnuts

6 to 8 servings

Arrange chicken in 3-quart casserole with thickest portions toward outside of casserole. Add celery, carrot, onion, ½ teaspoon thyme and water. Cover. Microwave at High for 16 to 20 minutes, or until chicken near bone is no longer pink, turning chicken over once. Skim fat. Strain and reserve broth. Set aside. Remove chicken from bones. Cut into bite-size pieces. Set aside.

Unwrap spinach and place on plate. Microwave at High for 4 to 5 minutes, or until defrosted. Drain thoroughly, pressing to remove excess moisture. Set aside.

Place butter in 2-quart casserole. Microwave at High for 45 seconds to 1 minute, or until butter melts. Stir in flour, salt, pepper, nutmeg and ⅛ teaspoon thyme. Blend in reserved broth and milk. Reduce power to 70% (Medium High). Microwave for 13 to 18 minutes, or until mixture thickens slightly and bubbles, stirring 3 or 4 times. Stir in chicken, spinach and water chestnuts. Microwave at 70% (Medium High) for 3 minutes, or until soup is heated through.

Turkey & Wild Rice Soup ▲

1 tablespoon butter or
   margarine
⅓ cup chopped carrot
⅛ teaspoon dried thyme leaves
   Dash dried marjoram leaves
1 tablespoon all-purpose flour
¼ teaspoon salt
1 cup ready-to-serve chicken
   broth
½ cup milk
2 egg yolks, slightly beaten
½ cup cut-up cooked turkey
⅓ cup cooked wild rice

4 to 6 servings

In 1½-quart casserole, combine butter, carrot, thyme and
marjoram. Cover. Microwave at
High for 3 to 7 minutes, or until
carrot is tender-crisp. Stir in
flour and salt. Blend in broth,
milk and egg yolks. Stir in
turkey and wild rice. Reduce
power to 70% (Medium High).
Microwave, uncovered, for 6 to
9 minutes, or just until mixture
thickens and bubbles, stirring
2 or 3 times.

Chicken & Wild Rice Soup:
Follow recipe above, substituting chicken for turkey.

Turkey Chili with Cheesy Dumplings

½ lb. ground turkey
⅔ cup chopped onion
¼ cup finely chopped celery
1 can (16 oz.) whole
   tomatoes, cut-up
1½ cups vegetable juice
   cocktail
1 can (8 oz.) kidney beans,
   drained
1¼ teaspoons chili powder
¾ teaspoon salt
½ teaspoon sugar
⅛ teaspoon garlic powder
⅛ teaspoon pepper

Cheesy Dumplings:
¾ cup all-purpose flour
3 tablespoons yellow
   cornmeal
   Dash ground oregano
¼ cup finely shredded
   Cheddar cheese
6 tablespoons milk

6 servings

Crumble turkey into 2-quart casserole. Add onion and celery.
Cover. Microwave at High for 3 to 5½ minutes, or until turkey is firm,
stirring after every 2 minutes to break apart turkey. Stir in remaining
soup ingredients. Re-cover. Microwave at High for 15 to 22 minutes,
or until flavors are blended, stirring 2 or 3 times.

In small mixing bowl, combine all Cheesy Dumpling ingredients. Stir
just until dry ingredients are moistened. For each dumpling,
measure about 2 tablespoons dough. Drop dumplings into hot
soup. Cover. Reduce power to 70% (Medium High). Microwave for
3 to 5 minutes, or until dumplings are set and no longer doughy,
rotating dish once.

Meatball & Eggplant Stew

Meatballs:

- ½ lb. ground turkey
- 1 egg
- 2 tablespoons seasoned dry bread crumbs
- 1 tablespoon minced green onion
- 1 tablespoon chili sauce
- 2 teaspoons snipped fresh parsley
- ¼ teaspoon salt
  Dash pepper

- 1½ cups peeled cubed eggplant, ½-inch cubes
- ½ cup chopped green pepper
- 2 tablespoons sliced green onion
- 1 tablespoon snipped fresh parsley
- 1 tablespoon olive oil
- ¾ teaspoon Italian seasoning
- 1 can (16 oz.) whole tomatoes, cut-up
- 1½ cups water
- 1 teaspoon instant beef bouillon granules
- ½ teaspoon salt
- ¼ teaspoon sugar
  Dash pepper

4 to 6 servings

In small mixing bowl, combine all meatball ingredients. Mix well. Shape into 15 meatballs, about 1¼ inches. Place meatballs in 2-quart casserole. Cover. Microwave at High for 3½ to 5 minutes, or until firm, rearranging meatballs once. Place meatballs on plate. Set aside.

In same casserole, combine eggplant, green pepper, onion, parsley, olive oil and Italian seasoning. Cover. Microwave at High for 5 to 7 minutes, or until vegetables are tender, stirring once. Add meatballs and remaining ingredients. Mix well. Re-cover. Reduce power to 70% (Medium High). Microwave for 10 to 15 minutes, or until hot, stirring once. Serve with Parmesan cheese.

◄ Turkey Stew

3 tablespoons butter or
   margarine
½ cup coarsely chopped onion
½ cup sliced carrot, ¼ inch
   thick
¼ cup all-purpose flour
2 cups water
2 cups coarsely shredded
   cabbage
1 to 1½ cups cut-up cooked
   turkey
1 can (10¾ oz.) condensed
   chicken broth
½ cup julienne yellow squash
   (2 × ¼-inch strips)
¼ cup frozen peas
¾ teaspoon salt
¼ teaspoon dried rosemary
   leaves, crushed
⅛ teaspoon pepper

4 to 6 servings

In 2-quart casserole, combine
butter, onion and carrot. Cover.
Microwave at High for 4 to
6 minutes, or until carrot is
tender-crisp, stirring once. Stir
in flour. Blend in water. Stir in
remaining ingredients. Re-cover.
Microwave at High for 15 to
23 minutes, or until cabbage is
tender and stew is slightly
thickened, stirring after every
5 minutes.

Chicken Stew: Follow recipe
above, substituting chicken
for turkey. Substitute 1 can
(10½ oz.) condensed chicken
and rice soup for chicken broth.

Smoked Turkey & ▲ Shrimp Soup

6 oz. medium shrimp, cut in
   half lengthwise
4 oz. smoked cooked turkey,
   cut into 1½ × ¼-inch strips
1 teaspoon cornstarch
4 cups ready-to-serve chicken
   broth
1 cup shredded lettuce
¼ cup bamboo shoots, cut into
   ⅛-inch strips
2 tablespoons sliced green
   onion
½ teaspoon salt
¼ teaspoon garlic powder
¼ teaspoon ground ginger
¼ teaspoon sesame oil

4 to 6 servings

In 2-quart casserole, combine
shrimp, turkey and cornstarch.
Toss to coat. Stir in remaining
ingredients. Microwave at 70%
(Medium High) for 9 to 13 minutes, or until shrimp are
opaque, stirring after every
3 minutes.

Smoked Turkey & Onion Soup

2 tablespoons butter or
   margarine
2 medium onions, sliced and
   separated into rings
1 clove garlic, minced
3 tablespoons white wine or
   apple juice
1½ cups ready-to-serve
   chicken broth
4 oz. smoked cooked turkey,
   cut into ¼-inch cubes
½ cup beef broth
¼ teaspoon salt
¼ teaspoon paprika
   Dash pepper
   Dairy sour cream (optional)

3 to 4 servings

In 1½-quart casserole, combine
butter, onion, garlic and wine.
Cover. Microwave at High for
9 to 13 minutes, or until onions
are tender and translucent,
stirring once or twice. Stir in
remaining ingredients, except
sour cream. Re-cover. Microwave at High for 5 to 6 minutes,
or until heated through, stirring
once. Garnish with sour cream.

Red Snapper ▶
& Clam Soup

1 tablespoon vegetable oil
½ cup chopped red onion
½ cup chopped celery
½ teaspoon ground coriander
¼ teaspoon grated lime peel
    Dash to ⅛ teaspoon cayenne
2 cups fresh broccoli flowerets
    and thinly sliced stalk
2 cups water
1 can (10 oz.) boiled baby
    clams, undrained
2 teaspoons fresh lime juice
1 teaspoon instant chicken
    bouillon granules
½ teaspoon salt
8 oz. red snapper fillets, about
    ¾ inch thick, cut into 1-inch
    pieces

6 servings

In 2-quart casserole, combine
oil, onion, celery, coriander, lime
peel and cayenne. Cover. Microwave at High for 4 to 5 minutes,
or until onion is tender, stirring
once. Stir in remaining ingredients, except red snapper.
Re-cover. Microwave at High for
7 to 9 minutes, or until broccoli
is tender-crisp, stirring once.
Quickly stir in red snapper.
Re-cover. Let stand for 3 to
5 minutes, or until fish flakes
easily with fork.

Cod & Vegetable Stew ▲

1 pkg. (12 oz.) frozen cod
    fillets
2 tablespoons olive oil
2 medium potatoes, cut into
    ½-inch cubes
1 medium red pepper, cut into
    ½-inch cubes
1 medium onion, cut in half
    lengthwise and thinly sliced

½ teaspoon dried thyme leaves
¼ teaspoon garlic powder
¾ teaspoon salt
1 can (14½ oz.) stewed
    tomatoes
1 bottle (8 oz.) clam juice
1 cup apple juice
1 cup frozen Italian green
    beans

8 servings

Place cod in 9-inch square baking dish. Microwave at 50%
(Medium) for 3 to 5 minutes, or until almost defrosted, breaking
apart after half the time. Let stand until completely defrosted. Set
aside. In 3-quart casserole, combine olive oil, potatoes, red pepper,
onion, thyme and garlic powder. Cover. Microwave at High for 8 to
9 minutes, or until potatoes are tender, stirring twice. Cut cod into
1-inch pieces. Add cod and remaining ingredients to potato mixture.
Re-cover. Microwave at High for 8 to 10 minutes, or until fish flakes
easily with fork, stirring 2 or 3 times. Serve with garlic toast.

◄ Mediterranean Fish Stew

2 tablespoons olive oil
1 leek, thinly sliced, about ¾ cup
½ cup chopped green pepper
1 clove garlic, minced
¼ teaspoon dried basil leaves
¼ teaspoon turmeric
⅛ teaspoon fennel seed, crushed
1½ cups water
1½ cups tomato juice
½ cup sliced zucchini, ¼ inch thick
1 teaspoon instant vegetable bouillon granules
½ teaspoon sugar
½ teaspoon salt
2 slices orange
1 bay leaf
1 lb. cod fillets, about ¾ inch thick, cut into 1-inch pieces

4 to 6 servings

In 2-quart casserole, combine olive oil, leek, green pepper, garlic, basil, turmeric and fennel. Cover. Microwave at High for 4 to 6 minutes, or until vegetables are tender, stirring once. Stir in remaining ingredients, except cod. Re-cover. Microwave at High for 10 to 15 minutes, or until zucchini is tender-crisp, stirring once. Remove orange slices and bay leaf. Gently stir in cod. Re-cover. Microwave at High for 3 to 4 minutes, or until fish flakes easily with fork, stirring after half the time.

Cream of Salmon Soup

3 tablespoons butter or margarine
⅓ cup chopped fresh mushrooms
2 tablespoons chopped onion
⅛ teaspoon dried tarragon leaves
2 tablespoons all-purpose flour

1 tablespoon snipped fresh parsley
2 teaspoons Dijon mustard
½ teaspoon salt
¼ teaspoon pepper
1½ cups milk
1 can (7½ oz.) salmon, drained and flaked

4 to 6 servings

In 1-quart casserole, combine butter, mushrooms, onion and tarragon. Cover. Microwave at High for 2 to 3 minutes, or until onion is tender. Stir in flour, parsley, mustard, salt and pepper. Blend in milk. Reduce power to 70% (Medium High). Microwave, uncovered, for 6 to 9 minutes, or until mixture thickens and bubbles, stirring 2 or 3 times. Remove bones and skin from salmon. Gently stir in salmon. Microwave at 70% (Medium High) for 1 minute, or until heated through.

Orange Roughy & Carrot Soup

8 oz. orange roughy fillets
2 tablespoons butter or
   margarine
3 cups thinly sliced carrots
¼ cup chopped onion
¼ teaspoon ground ginger
⅔ cup orange juice
1 can (14½ oz.) ready-to-serve
   chicken broth
¾ teaspoon salt
¼ cup sliced green onions

4 servings

Place orange roughy in 9-inch square baking dish. Cover with plastic wrap. Microwave at High for 3 to 4 minutes, or until fish flakes easily with fork, turning fillets over after half the time. Set aside. In 2-quart casserole, combine butter, carrots, chopped onion and ginger. Cover. Microwave at High for 8 to 13 minutes, or until carrots are very tender, stirring after every 2 minutes. In food processor or blender container, combine carrot mixture and orange juice. Process until mixture is smooth. Return mixture to 2-quart casserole. Stir in broth and salt. Cut orange roughy into bite-size pieces. Stir into soup. Cover. Microwave at High for 3 to 7 minutes, or until heated through, stirring gently after every 2 minutes. Sprinkle each serving with green onions.

Hot & Sour Fish Soup

  1 pkg. (6 oz.) frozen pea pods
  4 cups water
  ½ cup chopped onion
10 fresh mushrooms, cut in half
  1 clove garlic, minced
  3 tablespoons white wine
     vinegar
  1 tablespoon soy sauce
  1 teaspoon instant chicken
     bouillon granules
  1 teaspoon packed brown
     sugar
  ½ teaspoon salt
  ¼ teaspoon dried crushed red
     pepper
  ¼ teaspoon grated lime peel
  3 tablespoons cornstarch
  3 tablespoons cold water
12 oz. sole fillets, about ¼ inch
     thick, cut into 1-inch pieces
     Shredded carrot (optional)

6 to 8 servings

Unwrap pea pods and place on plate. Microwave at High for 2 minutes, or until defrosted. Set aside.

In 3-quart casserole, combine 4 cups water, onion, mushrooms, garlic, vinegar, soy sauce, bouillon, brown sugar, salt, red pepper and lime peel. Cover. Microwave at High for 10 to 15 minutes, or until mixture boils. In small bowl, blend cornstarch and cold water. Blend into hot mixture. Microwave, uncovered, at High for 5 to 10 minutes, or until mixture thickens and bubbles, stirring 2 or 3 times. Stir in pea pods and sole. Cover. Microwave at High for 2 to 3 minutes, or until fish flakes easily with fork. Garnish with shredded carrot.

Fish Chowder

Poaching Broth:

    2 cups water
    ¼ cup snipped fresh parsley
    1 tablespoon lemon juice
    1 teaspoon instant chicken
       bouillon granules
    ½ teaspoon salt
    ¼ teaspoon dried thyme
       leaves
    ⅛ teaspoon celery seed
   10 whole peppercorns
    4 whole allspice

   12 oz. flounder fillets, about
       ¼ inch thick
    1 cup cubed potatoes,
       ½-inch cubes
    ¼ cup chopped carrot
    ¼ cup chopped onion
    1 tablespoon water
    1 cup milk
    1 tablespoon capers, drained

                    4 to 6 servings

In 10-inch square casserole,
combine all poaching broth
ingredients. Cover. Microwave
at High for 7 to 13 minutes, or
until mixture boils. Add flounder
fillets. Re-cover. Reduce power
to 50% (Medium). Microwave
for 2 to 5 minutes, or until fish
flakes easily with fork. Remove
fish from broth and flake. Set
aside. Strain broth. Set aside.

In 1½-quart casserole, combine
potatoes, carrot and onion.
Sprinkle with water. Cover.
Microwave at High for 5 to
9 minutes, or until potatoes are
tender, stirring once. Stir in milk
and capers. Add poaching
broth and flounder. Re-cover.
Reduce power to 70% (Medium
High). Microwave for 5 to 8 minutes, or until heated through.

Shellfish Louisianne

1 pkg. (9 oz.) frozen
  artichoke hearts
2 tablespoons olive oil
2 cloves garlic, minced
1½ cups sliced fresh
  mushrooms
1 small zucchini, cut in half
  lengthwise, sliced ¼ inch
  thick
1 red or green pepper, cut
  into thin strips
½ cup thinly sliced carrot
1½ cups hot water
1 can (10½ oz.) condensed
  French onion soup
1 can (8 oz.) whole tomatoes,
  drained
2 teaspoons instant chicken
  bouillon granules
½ teaspoon salt
¼ teaspoon cayenne
1 can (8 oz.) whole baby
  oysters, drained
½ lb. bay scallops
3 to 4 cut-up seafood sticks

8 to 10 servings

Unwrap artichoke hearts and
place on plate. Microwave at
High for 4 to 5 minutes, or until
defrosted. Drain. Cut into bite-
size pieces. Set aside.

In 3-quart casserole, combine
olive oil and garlic. Cover. Microwave at High for 1 minute. Add
artichokes, mushrooms, zucchini,
red pepper, carrot, water, soup,
tomatoes, bouillon, salt and
cayenne. Stir. Re-cover. Microwave at High for 10 minutes,
stirring once or twice. Reduce
power to 50% (Medium). Microwave for 8 to 12 minutes, or until
vegetables are just tender-crisp.
Add oysters, scallops and
seafood sticks. Stir gently.
Re-cover. Microwave at 50%
(Medium) for 5 to 8 minutes, or
until scallops are opaque. Serve
with French bread.

Summer Shrimp & ▲ Tarragon Soup

2 tablespoons butter or
  margarine
1 cup sliced fresh mushrooms
1 cup julienne zucchini
  (1½ × ¼-inch strips)
2 tablespoons sliced green
  onion
1 tablespoon snipped fresh
  parsley
1 can (10¾ oz.) condensed
  chicken broth
1 cup water
⅓ cup white wine
¼ teaspoon salt
¼ teaspoon dried tarragon
  leaves
⅛ teaspoon pepper
½ lb. small shrimp, shelled and
  deveined

4 servings

In 1½-quart casserole, combine
butter, mushrooms, zucchini,
onion and parsley. Microwave at
High for 3 to 5 minutes, or until
zucchini is tender-crisp, stirring
once. Stir in remaining ingredients, except shrimp. Microwave
at High for 7 to 9 minutes, or
until mixture boils. Stir in shrimp.
Reduce power to 50% (Medium).
Microwave for 3 to 4 minutes,
or until shrimp are opaque,
stirring once.

Saffron Shrimp Soup

1 pkg. (12 oz.) frozen
  ready-to-cook shrimp
2 tablespoons butter or
  margarine
1 cup cubed potatoes, ¼-inch
  cubes
½ cup grated carrots
1 clove garlic, minced
¼ teaspoon saffron threads or
  ⅛ teaspoon turmeric
3 tablespoons all-purpose flour
¾ teaspoon salt
2 cups half-and-half
1 cup chicken broth
2 medium tomatoes, seeded
  and chopped

6 to 8 servings

Place shrimp in single layer
in 9-inch round baking dish.
Microwave at 50% (Medium)
for 3½ to 6 minutes, or until
defrosted, stirring twice. Let
stand for 3 minutes. Set aside.
In 2-quart casserole, combine
butter, potatoes, carrots, garlic
and saffron. Cover. Microwave
at High for 3 to 5 minutes, or
until potatoes are tender. Stir in
flour and salt. Blend in half-and-
half and broth. Add shrimp and
tomatoes. Reduce power to
50% (Medium). Microwave,
uncovered, for 17 to 25 minutes,
or until shrimp are opaque,
stirring after every 5 minutes.

Tomato-Tarragon Lobster Soup

- 3 tablespoons butter or margarine, divided
- 1 clove garlic, minced
- ¼ teaspoon dried tarragon leaves
- 1 can (16 oz.) whole tomatoes, cut-up
- 1 teaspoon sugar
- ½ teaspoon salt
- ⅛ teaspoon pepper
- 1 tablespoon all-purpose flour
- 1½ cups milk
- ¼ lb. cut-up cooked lobster or mock lobster

4 servings

In medium mixing bowl, combine 2 tablespoons butter, garlic and tarragon. Cover with plastic wrap. Microwave at High for 3 to 4 minutes, or until butter melts and garlic is lightly browned. Stir in tomatoes, sugar, salt and pepper. Re-cover. Microwave at High for 1½ to 3 minutes, or until heated through. Set aside.

Place remaining 1 tablespoon butter in 2-quart casserole. Microwave at High for 45 seconds to 1 minute, or until butter melts. Stir in flour. Blend in milk. Microwave at High for 4 to 6½ minutes, or until mixture thickens and bubbles, stirring after every 2 minutes. Stir tomato mixture into milk mixture. Stir in lobster. Cover. Let stand for 1 minute.

Cold Curried Crab Soup

- 1 pkg. (3 oz.) cream cheese
- 1 tablespoon butter or margarine
- 2 medium potatoes, cut into ½-inch cubes, about 2 cups
- ½ cup chopped carrot
- ¼ cup chopped celery
- ½ teaspoon curry powder
- ⅛ teaspoon ground cinnamon
- 1 cup ready-to-serve chicken broth
- ¾ cup half-and-half
- ½ teaspoon salt
- ⅛ teaspoon cayenne
- 1 pkg. (6 oz.) frozen crab meat, defrosted, drained and cartilage removed
  Snipped fresh chives (optional)

4 servings

Place cream cheese in small bowl. Microwave at 50% (Medium) for 30 seconds to 1 minute, or until softened. Set aside. In 2-quart casserole, combine butter, potatoes, carrot, celery, curry powder and cinnamon. Cover. Microwave at High for 7 to 8 minutes, or until vegetables are very tender, stirring after half the time. In food processor or blender container, combine vegetable mixture, cream cheese, broth, half-and-half, salt and cayenne. Process until mixture is smooth. Stir in crab meat. Cover. Chill for at least 2 hours, or until cold. Garnish with chives.

Crab Bisque ▲

- 3 slices bacon, cut into 1-inch pieces
- ½ cup chopped red or green pepper
- 2 tablespoons sliced green onion
- 1 clove garlic, minced
- 3 tablespoons all-purpose flour
- 1½ cups water
- 1 cup evaporated milk
- ¾ cup frozen corn
- 1 can (6 oz.) crab meat, rinsed, drained and cartilage removed
- ½ teaspoon salt
- ¼ teaspoon dried crushed sage leaves
  Dash cayenne

4 servings

Place bacon in 1½-quart casserole. Cover. Microwave at High for 4 to 6 minutes, or until bacon is crisp. Drain, reserving 2 tablespoons bacon fat. Place bacon in small dish. Set aside. In same casserole, combine reserved bacon fat, red pepper, onion and garlic. Re-cover. Microwave at High for 2 to 3 minutes, or until pepper is tender-crisp, stirring once. Stir in flour. Blend in bacon and remaining ingredients. Microwave, uncovered, at High for 7 to 10 minutes, or until mixture thickens and bubbles, stirring twice.

Spinach & Crab Soup

- 1 pkg. (10 oz.) frozen chopped spinach
- 3 tablespoons butter or margarine
- ¼ cup chopped onion
- ¼ cup chopped celery
- 3 tablespoons all-purpose flour
- 2 cups half-and-half
- 1 can (14½ oz.) ready-to-serve chicken broth
- 1 pkg. (6 oz.) frozen crab meat, defrosted, drained and cartilage removed
- ½ teaspoon salt
- ⅛ teaspoon ground mace
- 2 tablespoons dry sherry (optional)

4 to 6 servings

Unwrap spinach and place on plate. Microwave at High for 4 to 5 minutes, or until defrosted. Let stand for 5 minutes.

Drain thoroughly, pressing to remove excess moisture. Set aside.

In 2-quart casserole, combine butter, onion and celery. Cover. Microwave at High for 3 to 4 minutes, or until vegetables are tender, stirring once. Stir in flour. Blend in remaining ingredients, except sherry. Re-cover. Reduce power to 50% (Medium). Microwave for 20 to 26 minutes, or until hot, stirring 3 times. Stir in sherry.

Spinach & Seafood Soup:
Follow recipe above, substituting cut-up seafood sticks for crab meat.

Oyster Chowder ▶

    3 tablespoons butter or
        margarine
  ½ cup chopped onion
    1 clove garlic, minced
  ½ teaspoon dried basil leaves
  ¼ teaspoon dried thyme
        leaves
    2 tablespoons all-purpose
        flour
  ½ teaspoon salt
  ⅛ teaspoon white pepper
1½ cups half-and-half
    1 can (8 oz.) whole baby
        oysters, drained
    4 to 6 drops hot pepper
        sauce
  ⅓ cup white wine
    1 medium tomato, seeded
        and chopped

4 servings

In 1½-quart casserole, combine
butter, onion, garlic, basil and
thyme. Cover. Microwave at High
for 2 to 4 minutes, or until onion
is tender. Stir in flour, salt and
pepper. Blend in half-and-half.
Stir in oysters and hot pepper
sauce. Reduce power to 70%
(Medium High). Microwave,
uncovered, for 8 to 12 minutes,
or until mixture thickens and
bubbles, stirring 2 or 3 times.
Blend in wine. Stir in tomato.
Let stand, covered, for 1 minute.

Dilly Clam Soup ▲

    2 tablespoons butter or
        margarine
  ½ cup cubed potato, ½-inch
        cubes
  ⅓ cup chopped celery
  ¼ cup chopped onion
  ¼ cup cubed fully cooked ham
  ⅛ teaspoon dried dill weed
        Dash dried summer savory
        leaves
1¾ cups water

    1 can (6½ oz.) minced
        clams, undrained
    1 tablespoon diced pimiento,
        drained
    1 teaspoon lemon juice
  ¾ teaspoon instant chicken
        bouillon granules
  ¼ teaspoon salt
    4 to 5 drops hot pepper
        sauce

3 to 4 servings

In 1-quart casserole, combine butter, potato, celery, onion, ham, dill
and summer savory. Cover. Microwave at High for 5 to 8 minutes,
or until potato is tender, stirring once. Stir in remaining ingredients.
Re-cover. Microwave at High for 3 to 6 minutes, or until heated
through, stirring once. Serve with oyster crackers.

Marinated Chicken ▶ & Bean Salad

1 pkg. (9 oz.) frozen artichoke hearts
1 boneless whole chicken breast (8 to 10 oz.) skin removed, cut into 1-inch cubes
½ cup chopped onion
1 clove garlic, minced
⅛ teaspoon dried crushed sage leaves
⅛ teaspoon dried thyme leaves
1 can (16 oz.) Great Northern beans, rinsed and drained
⅓ cup chopped red pepper
1 tablespoon snipped fresh parsley

Dressing:
3 tablespoons olive oil
2 tablespoons white wine vinegar
1 teaspoon salt
Dash cayenne

6 to 8 servings

Unwrap artichoke hearts and place in 2-quart casserole. Cover. Microwave at High for 3 to 4 minutes, or until slightly warm, stirring after half the time to break apart. Add chicken, onion, garlic, sage and thyme. Re-cover. Microwave at High for 4 to 6½ minutes, or until chicken is no longer pink, stirring twice. Drain. Place chicken mixture in large mixing bowl. Stir in beans, red pepper and parsley. In 1-cup measure, blend all dressing ingredients. Pour over chicken mixture. Toss to coat. Cover. Chill for at least 3 hours before serving.

Mediterranean Chicken Salad ▲

2½ to 3-lb. broiler-fryer chicken, cut into 4 pieces
1 teaspoon dried oregano leaves
½ teaspoon salt
¼ teaspoon pepper
½ cup red wine
2 cups peeled cubed eggplant, ½-inch cubes
½ cup chopped red onion
1 clove garlic, minced
2 medium tomatoes, seeded and chopped
⅓ cup sliced black olives

Dressing:
3 tablespoons olive oil
2 tablespoons lemon juice
1 tablespoon snipped fresh parsley
¾ teaspoon salt
½ teaspoon dried oregano leaves
¼ teaspoon sugar
¼ teaspoon pepper

6 servings

Arrange chicken in shallow 3-quart casserole with thickest portions toward outside of casserole. Sprinkle with oregano, salt and pepper. Pour wine over chicken. Cover. Microwave at High for 16 to 22 minutes, or until chicken near bone is no longer pink and juices run clear, turning chicken over after half the time. Remove chicken. Set aside.

Place 2 tablespoons cooking liquid from chicken in 2-quart casserole. Add eggplant, onion and garlic. Cover. Microwave at High for 5 to 7 minutes, or until eggplant is tender, stirring once. Remove chicken from bones. Cut into bite-size pieces. Add chicken, tomatoes and olives to eggplant mixture. In 1-cup measure, combine all dressing ingredients. Mix well. Pour over chicken and vegetables. Toss to coat. Cover. Chill for at least 3 hours before serving.

Hot Chicken Waldorf in Puff Pastry Shells

1 can (6¾ oz.) chunk chicken, drained
⅔ cup chopped apple
½ cup shredded Swiss cheese
½ cup mayonnaise
2 tablespoons finely chopped celery
2 tablespoons sunflower nuts
1 tablespoon sliced green onion
1 teaspoon lemon juice
¼ teaspoon lemon pepper seasoning
6 baked individual pastry shells

6 servings

In 1-quart casserole, combine all ingredients, except pastry shells. Mix well. Microwave at High for 2½ to 4 minutes, or until mixture is hot and cheese melts, stirring twice. Spoon chicken mixture into puff pastry shells.

Hot Chicken Waldorf Sandwiches: Follow recipe above, except substitute 6 whole wheat hamburger buns, split, for pastry shells. Combine chicken mixture in small mixing bowl. Arrange bottom half of buns on paper towel-lined platter. Top each with about ⅓ cup chicken mixture. Microwave at High for 3 to 5 minutes, or until mixture is hot and cheese melts, rotating platter once. Top with remaining bun halves.

Tropical Chicken-Melon Salad

1 pkg. (7 oz.) uncooked spaghetti
2 slices bacon, cut-up
1 boneless whole chicken breast (8 to 10 oz.) skin removed, cut into ¾-inch cubes
1 small onion, thinly sliced
½ teaspoon dried marjoram leaves
½ teaspoon salt
⅓ cup mayonnaise
2 cups cubed cantaloupe, ¾-inch cubes
1 avocado, cut into ¾-inch cubes

4 to 6 servings

Cook spaghetti as directed on package. Drain. Set aside. Place bacon in 2-quart casserole. Microwave at High for 2½ to 3½ minutes, or until bacon is crisp, stirring 1 or 2 times. Remove bacon with slotted spoon. Set aside. In same casserole, combine bacon fat, chicken, onion, marjoram and salt. Mix well. Cover. Microwave at High for 3½ to 4 minutes, or until chicken is no longer pink, stirring after every 2 minutes. Drain. Reserve liquid. In small mixing bowl, combine reserved liquid, mayonnaise and bacon. Pour mayonnaise mixture over spaghetti. Toss to coat. Add cantaloupe to chicken mixture. Serve spaghetti topped with cantaloupe and chicken mixture. Top with avocado.

Turkey & Spinach Salad ▲

¾ lb. fresh spinach, trimmed
    and torn into bite-size
    pieces, about 6 cups
1 can (11 oz.) mandarin
    oranges, drained
1 cup fresh bean sprouts
8 oz. smoked turkey, cut into
    3 × ¼-inch strips
½ cup walnut halves
2 slices bacon, cut-up
    Vegetable oil
3 tablespoons cider vinegar
1 teaspoon freeze-dried chives
¼ teaspoon onion salt
¼ teaspoon dry mustard
    Dash pepper

6 to 8 servings

In large mixing bowl, layer
spinach, oranges, bean sprouts,
turkey and walnuts. Set aside.
Place bacon in 2-cup measure.
Microwave at High for 2½ to 3½
minutes, or until crisp, stirring
1 or 2 times. Remove bacon
with slotted spoon. Reserve
bacon fat. Add bacon to salad
mixture. Set aside. Add vegetable oil to bacon fat to equal
¼ cup. Stir in remaining ingredients. Microwave at High for
30 to 45 seconds, or until hot.
Stir to blend. Pour over salad.
Toss to coat.

Salmon Potato Salad

2 baking potatoes (8 oz. each)
    cut into ½-inch cubes
¼ cup sliced green onions
1 tablespoon snipped fresh
    parsley
1 tablespoon olive oil
½ teaspoon salt
¼ teaspoon dried dill weed
¼ teaspoon grated lemon peel

1 pkg. (10 oz.) frozen
    asparagus cuts
1 can (7½ oz.) salmon,
    drained and flaked
⅓ cup mayonnaise
2 tablespoons dairy sour
    cream
2 teaspoons Dijon mustard

4 servings

In 2-quart casserole, combine potatoes, onions, parsley, olive oil, salt,
dill and lemon peel. Cover. Microwave at High for 7 to 10 minutes,
or until potatoes are tender, stirring after every 3 minutes. Set aside.

Unwrap asparagus and place in 1-quart casserole. Cover. Microwave at High for 3 to 4 minutes, or until defrosted, stirring after half
the time to break apart. Drain. Add to potato mixture. Remove
bones and skin from salmon. Combine salmon with potato mixture.
Mix well. In small mixing bowl, blend mayonnaise, sour cream and
mustard. Spoon dressing over each serving of salad.

◄ Lobster Rice Salad

1½ cups hot water
⅔ cup uncooked long-grain white rice
2 tablespoons chopped onion
1 tablespoon snipped fresh parsley
¾ teaspoon grated lemon peel
½ teaspoon salt
½ teaspoon instant chicken bouillon granules
¼ teaspoon dried dill weed
1 cup cut-up cooked lobster
1 medium tomato, seeded and chopped
⅓ cup sliced celery

Dressing:

¼ cup vegetable oil
1 tablespoon white wine vinegar
1 teaspoon lemon juice
¼ teaspoon salt
¼ teaspoon sugar
¼ teaspoon dry mustard
Dash pepper

4 servings

In 2-quart casserole, combine water, rice, onion, parsley, lemon peel, salt, bouillon and dill. Cover. Microwave at High for 5 minutes. Reduce power to 70% (Medium High). Microwave for 12 to 19 minutes, or until liquid is absorbed and rice is tender. Let stand, covered, for 5 minutes. Cool slightly.

Combine lobster, tomato and celery with rice mixture. Set aside. In small mixing bowl, blend all dressing ingredients. Pour over lobster and rice mixture. Toss to coat. Re-cover. Chill for 2 to 3 hours.

Seafood Louis Salad

Dressing:

1 tablespoon butter or margarine
2 tablespoons sliced green onion
2 tablespoons chopped green pepper
⅛ teaspoon cayenne
⅔ cup mayonnaise
¼ cup chili sauce
¼ cup whipping cream
1 tablespoon ketchup
½ teaspoon Worcestershire sauce

Salad:

½ lb. large shrimp, shelled and deveined
½ lb. sea scallops
¼ teaspoon grated lemon peel
6 cups trimmed and torn lettuce
¼ lb. cooked crab meat
1 medium tomato, cut into wedges
Lemon slices (optional)
Hard-cooked eggs (optional)
Black olives (optional)

6 servings

In 1-quart casserole, combine butter, onion, green pepper and cayenne. Cover. Microwave at High for 1 to 2½ minutes, or until vegetables are tender-crisp. Stir in remaining dressing ingredients. Re-cover. Chill while preparing salad.

In 2-quart casserole, combine shrimp, scallops and lemon peel. Cover. Microwave at 70% (Medium High) for 5 to 7½ minutes, or until shrimp and scallops are opaque, stirring 2 or 3 times. Rinse with cold water. Drain. Place lettuce on serving platter. Arrange shrimp, scallops, crab meat and tomato on lettuce. Garnish with lemon slices, hard-cooked eggs and olives. Serve with dressing.

◄ Garden Salad with Cod

12 oz. cod fillets, cut into
    serving-size pieces
¼ cup white wine
1 small onion, thinly sliced
1 clove garlic, minced
3 tablespoons vegetable oil
¾ teaspoon salt
¼ teaspoon fennel seed,
    crushed
⅛ teaspoon dried crushed red
    pepper
1 pkg. (10 oz.) frozen mixed
    vegetables
4 cups trimmed and torn
    lettuce or spinach
2 tablespoons white wine
    vinegar

4 to 6 servings

In 9-inch round baking dish,
combine cod and wine. Cover.
Microwave at High for 3½ to
5½ minutes, or until fish flakes
easily with fork, turning pieces
over after half the time. Cool
slightly. Set aside.

In 1½-quart casserole, combine
onion, garlic, oil, salt, fennel and
red pepper. Cover. Microwave
at High for 2 to 4 minutes, or
until onion is tender. Add mixed
vegetables. Re-cover. Microwave at High for 4 to 6 minutes,
or until heated through, stirring
once to break apart.

Flake cod. In medium mixing
bowl, combine vegetable
mixture, cod and lettuce.
Sprinkle with vinegar. Toss to
coat. Cover. Chill for at least
1 hour before serving.

Shrimp Salad ▲

1 bag (12 oz.) frozen shrimp
    pieces
1 cup uncooked small shell
    macaroni
½ cup peeled, seeded and
    chopped cucumber
⅓ cup sliced black olives
2 tablespoons finely chopped
    green pepper

Dressing:
⅓ cup mayonnaise
2 tablespoons dairy sour
    cream
1½ teaspoons lemon juice
1 teaspoon grated onion
½ teaspoon salt
⅛ teaspoon dried dill weed
⅛ teaspoon pepper

4 to 6 servings

Place frozen shrimp in 2-quart casserole. Cover. Microwave at 70%
(Medium High) for 8 to 13 minutes, or until shrimp are opaque,
stirring 3 times. Drain. Rinse with cold water. Drain. Place in
medium mixing bowl. Set aside.

Cook macaroni as directed on package. Rinse with cold water.
Drain. Combine with shrimp. Stir in cucumber, olives and green
pepper. In small mixing bowl, blend all dressing ingredients. Pour
over shrimp and vegetables. Mix well. Cover. Chill for at least
2 hours before serving.

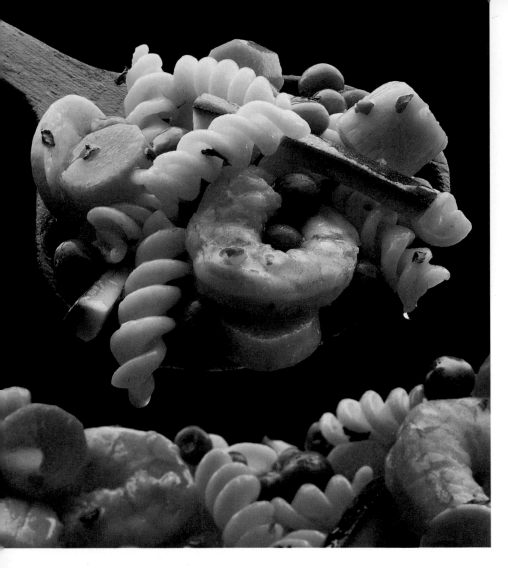

Tuna Niçoise

1 lb. new potatoes, thinly sliced
¼ cup olive oil
2 tablespoons red wine vinegar
1 tablespoon snipped fresh parsley
1 clove garlic, minced
½ teaspoon salt
¼ teaspoon dried thyme leaves
⅛ teaspoon pepper
1 pkg. (9 oz.) frozen whole green beans
6 to 8 cherry tomatoes, each cut into 4 pieces
¼ cup pitted black olives, cut in half
Lettuce leaves
1 can (7 oz.) albacore tuna, drained

4 servings

In 2-quart casserole, combine potatoes, olive oil, vinegar, parsley, garlic, salt, thyme and pepper. Cover. Microwave at High for 7 to 13 minutes, or until tender, stirring after every 3 minutes. Set aside.

Unwrap beans and place in 1-quart casserole. Cover. Microwave at High for 4 to 5 minutes, or until beans are hot, stirring after half the time to break apart. Drain. Add to potato mixture. Re-cover. Chill for 3 to 4 hours. Stir in tomatoes and olives. Arrange lettuce on serving platter. Place flaked tuna in center of lettuce-lined platter. Spoon potato mixture around tuna.

Seafood Pasta Salad ▲

½ cup sliced carrot, ¼ inch thick
½ cup frozen peas
6 tablespoons Italian dressing, divided
¼ lb. bay scallops
¼ lb. extra-small shrimp, shelled and deveined
¼ teaspoon dried basil leaves
1 cup sliced fresh mushrooms
½ cup julienne zucchini (2 × ¼-inch strips)
1 pkg. (7 oz.) uncooked rotini pasta
½ teaspoon salt
⅛ teaspoon pepper

6 to 8 servings

In 1-quart casserole, combine carrot, peas and ¼ cup dressing. Cover. Microwave at High for 2 to 3 minutes, or until colors brighten, stirring once. Set aside. In 9-inch square baking dish, combine scallops and shrimp. Sprinkle with basil. Cover with plastic wrap. Microwave at 70% (Medium High) for 3 to 5 minutes, or until scallops and shrimp are opaque, stirring once or twice. Drain. Combine shrimp and scallops with carrot mixture. Stir in mushrooms and zucchini. Re-cover. Chill for 1 hour.

Cook rotini as directed on package. Rinse with cold water. Drain. Place in large mixing bowl. Mix in seafood and vegetables. In small bowl, blend remaining 2 tablespoons dressing, salt and pepper. Pour over salad. Toss to coat. Re-cover. Chill for at least 2 hours before serving.

Curried Broccoli & Shrimp Salad

2 cups fresh broccoli flowerets
½ cup shredded carrots
1 small onion, thinly sliced
1 clove garlic, minced
2 tablespoons vegetable oil
1 tablespoon honey
½ teaspoon curry powder
¼ teaspoon caraway seed
¼ teaspoon salt
⅛ teaspoon cayenne
1 lb. large shrimp, shelled
   and deveined
⅓ cup cocktail peanuts

   4 servings

In 2-quart casserole, combine broccoli, carrots, onion and garlic. In small mixing bowl, combine oil, honey, curry powder, caraway, salt and cayenne. Pour over vegetables. Cover. Microwave at High for 5 to 6 minutes, or until vegetables are tender-crisp, stirring after half the time. Set aside.

Place shrimp in 1½-quart casserole. Cover. Microwave at 70% (Medium High) for 6 to 12 minutes, or until shrimp are opaque, stirring after every 2 minutes. Drain. Combine shrimp with vegetables. Re-cover. Chill for 3 to 4 hours, stirring once or twice. Stir in peanuts before serving.

Chicken Pizza Sandwiches

½ cup thinly sliced green pepper
1 small onion, thinly sliced
2 teaspoons olive oil
¼ teaspoon dried crushed red pepper
¼ teaspoon Italian seasoning
⅛ teaspoon garlic powder
⅛ teaspoon fennel seed, crushed
1 can (8 oz.) tomato sauce
¼ cup sliced black olives
1 cup shredded Cheddar cheese, divided
1 cup cut-up cooked chicken
2 pita breads, 6-inch

4 servings

In 2-quart casserole, combine green pepper, onion, olive oil, red pepper, Italian seasoning, garlic powder and fennel. Cover. Microwave at High for 2 to 4 minutes, or until vegetables are tender, stirring after half the time. Stir in tomato sauce and olives. Microwave, uncovered, at High for 4 to 5 minutes, or until hot, stirring after half the time. Stir in ½ cup Cheddar cheese and chicken.

Split each pita bread in half. Toast. Spoon one-fourth of chicken mixture onto each pita half. Sprinkle each with remaining ½ cup Cheddar cheese. Place 2 pita halves on paper towel-lined plate. Microwave at 50% (Medium) for 2 to 3 minutes, or until cheese melts, rotating plate after half the time. Repeat with remaining pita halves.

Smoked Cheese & ▶
Turkey Salad Sandwiches

- 4 slices bacon
- ¼ cup chopped onion
- ¼ cup chopped green pepper
- ¼ cup chopped celery
- 1 tablespoon butter or margarine
- 2 cups cubed cooked turkey, ½-inch cubes
- ½ cup cubed smoked Cheddar cheese, ¼-inch cubes
- ⅓ cup mayonnaise
- 1 teaspoon prepared mustard
- 1 teaspoon Worcestershire sauce
- 4 Kaiser rolls, 4-inch, unsplit

4 servings

Place bacon on paper towel-lined plate. Cover with paper towel. Microwave at High for 3½ to 6 minutes, or until crisp. Crumble. Set aside. In 2-quart casserole, combine onion, green pepper, celery and butter. Microwave at High for 2 to 4 minutes, or until vegetables are tender-crisp. Stir in turkey, bacon and cheese. In small mixing bowl, blend mayonnaise, mustard and Worcestershire sauce. Add to turkey mixture. Mix well.

Cut thin slice from top of each roll. Scoop out center of each roll to within ¼ inch of edge. Fill each roll with turkey mixture. Arrange rolls on paper towel-lined platter. Cover with wax paper. Microwave at 50% (Medium) for 3 to 4 minutes, or just until cheese begins to melt, rotating platter after every minute.

Patty Melts

- 1 lb. ground turkey
- 1 tablespoon finely chopped onion
- 1 tablespoon milk
- 1 teaspoon Worcestershire sauce
- ¼ teaspoon salt
- ¼ teaspoon pepper
- ⅛ teaspoon garlic powder
- 4 slices (¾ oz. each) pasteurized process American cheese
- 4 English muffins, split and toasted

4 servings

In medium mixing bowl, combine ground turkey, onion, milk, Worcestershire sauce, salt, pepper and garlic powder. Mix well. Shape into 4 patties, about ½ inch thick. Arrange patties on roasting rack. Microwave at High for 4 minutes. Turn patties over and rearrange. Microwave at High for 3 to 6 minutes, or until cooked through. Top with cheese slices. Reduce power to 50% (Medium). Microwave for 2 to 4 minutes, or until cheese melts. Serve in toasted English muffins with ketchup or mustard.

Turkey Tacos ▲

1 lb. ground turkey
¼ cup chopped onion
1 pkg. (1¼ oz.) taco
   seasoning mix
8 to 12 taco shells

Toppings:
   Shredded lettuce
   Chopped tomato
   Chopped black olives
   Shredded Cheddar cheese

6 to 8 servings

Crumble ground turkey into
1½-quart casserole. Stir in
onion. Microwave at High for
4 to 5 minutes, or until firm and
cooked through, stirring twice
to break apart. Drain. Stir in
seasoning mix and water as
directed on seasoning package.
Microwave at High for 5½ to
6½ minutes, or until mixture
thickens, stirring after every
2 minutes. Spoon into taco
shells. Serve with toppings.

Mustard Relish Dogs

Mustard Relish:
1 tablespoon sweet pickle
   relish
1 tablespoon chopped onion
1½ teaspoons prepared
   mustard
¼ teaspoon prepared
   horseradish

2 hot dog buns
2 large turkey wieners
   (2 oz. each)

2 servings

In small bowl, combine all
Mustard Relish ingredients. Mix
well. Spread on 1 side of each
hot dog bun. Place wiener in
each bun. Arrange on paper
towel-lined plate. Cover with
paper towel. Microwave at High
for 1½ to 2¾ minutes, or until
heated through, rotating once.

For 4 Mustard Relish Dogs,
follow recipe above, except
double all ingredients. Microwave at High for 2½ to
3½ minutes, or until heated
through, rotating plate once.

Greek Pita Sandwiches ▶

Yogurt Sauce:
1 carton (8 oz.) plain yogurt
2 green onions, sliced
½ teaspoon garlic salt
   Dash cayenne

Turkey Mixture:
½ lb. ground turkey
½ lb. ground lamb
1 clove garlic, minced
½ cup water
1 envelope (1¼ oz.) onion
   soup mix
1 tablespoon olive oil
2 teaspoons dried parsley
   flakes
½ teaspoon dried oregano
   leaves
¼ teaspoon cayenne
⅛ teaspoon ground allspice
⅛ teaspoon dried thyme leaves

4 pita breads, 6-inch

Toppings:
   Shredded lettuce
   Chopped cucumber
   Chopped tomato

4 servings

In small mixing bowl, combine
all Yogurt Sauce ingredients.
Mix well. Chill while preparing
turkey mixture.

Crumble ground turkey and
lamb into 2-quart casserole. Stir
in garlic. Microwave at High for
4 to 6 minutes, or until meat is
no longer pink, stirring after
every 2 minutes to break apart.
Drain. Stir in remaining turkey
mixture ingredients. Cover.
Microwave at High for 3 to
5 minutes, or until hot. Spoon
into pita breads. Serve with
Yogurt Sauce and toppings.

Mexican Meatball Hoagie

¾ cup shredded zucchini
¼ cup chopped green pepper
2 tablespoons chopped onion
4 bratwurst buns, split

Meatballs:

1 lb. ground turkey
3 tablespoons taco sauce
2 tablespoons finely chopped
    onion
1 teaspoon chili powder
½ teaspoon salt
¼ teaspoon pepper
⅛ teaspoon garlic powder
⅛ teaspoon ground cinnamon

⅔ cup taco sauce

4 servings

In small mixing bowl, combine zucchini, green pepper and onion. Mix well. Spoon mixture into bratwurst buns. Set aside. In medium mixing bowl, combine all meatball ingredients. Mix well. Shape into 16 meatballs, about 1½ inches. Place meatballs in 2-quart casserole. Cover. Microwave at High for 5 to 8 minutes, or until firm and cooked through, stirring gently to rearrange twice. Drain. Pour remaining ⅔ cup taco sauce over meatballs. Re-cover. Reduce power to 50% (Medium). Microwave for 2 to 3 minutes, or until heated through. Arrange 4 meatballs over zucchini mixture in each bun. Spoon sauce over meatballs.

Turkey Pockets

½ lb. ground turkey
2 slices bacon, cut-up
¼ teaspoon dried oregano
   leaves
⅓ cup chopped black olives
3 tablespoons chili sauce
2 large or 4 small pita breads
   Shredded lettuce

2 to 4 servings

Crumble ground turkey into
1-quart casserole. Microwave at
High for 2½ to 4½ minutes, or
until firm and cooked through,
stirring once to break apart.
Drain. Set aside. Place bacon in
same casserole. Microwave at
High for 2½ to 3½ minutes, or
until bacon is crisp, stirring 1 or
2 times. Sprinkle with oregano
when bacon just begins to
brown. Stir in turkey, olives and
chili sauce. Microwave at High
for 1 to 2 minutes, or until heated
through. Spoon into pita breads.
Top with shredded lettuce.

Pub Burgers ▲

½ lb. ground turkey
3 tablespoons French dressing
1 tablespoon coarse ground
   prepared mustard
1 teaspoon prepared
   horseradish

⅛ teaspoon dried dill weed
2 whole wheat hamburger
   buns, split and toasted
4 slices (¾ to 1 oz. each)
   sharp Cheddar cheese

4 servings

Crumble ground turkey into 1-quart casserole. Microwave at High
for 2½ to 4½ minutes, or until firm and cooked through, stirring
once to break apart. Drain. Stir in French dressing, mustard, horseradish and dill. Microwave at High for 1 to 2 minutes, or until heated
through. Arrange 4 toasted bun halves on paper towel-lined platter.
Spoon turkey mixture onto each bun half. Top each with Cheddar
cheese slice. Microwave at 70% (Medium High) for 1½ to 2½
minutes, or until cheese melts, rotating platter once or twice. Serve
burgers open-face.

Three-layer ▶ Luncheon Loaf

2 tablespoons butter or
  margarine
¼ cup chopped onion
¼ cup chopped carrot
¼ cup chopped green pepper
1 pkg. (8 oz.) cream cheese,
  cut into small pieces
⅓ cup mayonnaise
1 can (7½ oz.) salmon,
  drained and flaked
⅛ teaspoon dried dill weed
1 can (6¾ oz.) chunk chicken,
  drained
2 tablespoons sliced almonds
⅛ teaspoon garlic powder
1 can (4¼ oz.) small shrimp,
  drained
2 tablespoons chopped water
  chestnuts
1 lb. round flat sourdough
  bread, about 6½ × 4½
  inches

8 servings

How to Microwave Three-layer Luncheon Loaf

Combine butter, onion, carrot
and green pepper in 1-quart
casserole. Cover. Microwave at
High for 2½ to 3½ minutes, or
until vegetables are tender,
stirring after half the time. Add
cream cheese. Re-cover.

Reduce power to 50%
(Medium). Microwave for 1 to
2 minutes, or until softened. Stir
in mayonnaise until smooth.
Divide cream cheese mixture
into 3 equal parts. Place each
portion in small mixing bowl.
Set aside.

Remove bones and skin from
salmon. Combine salmon and
dill with one portion cream
cheese. Mix well. Set aside.

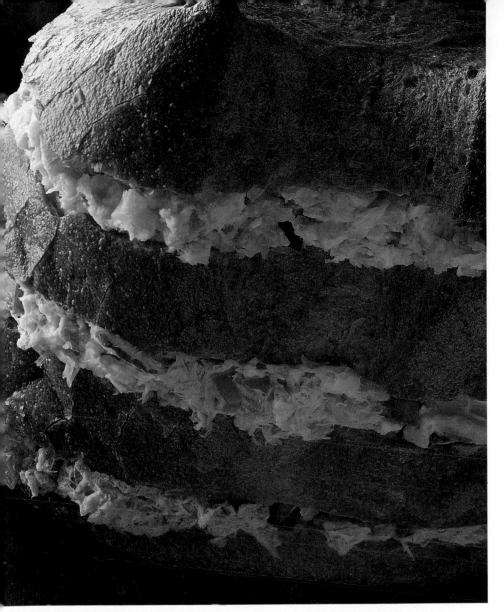

Oyster Denvers

2 teaspoons butter or margarine
2 tablespoons chopped green pepper
2 tablespoons sliced green onion
½ pint fresh oysters, well drained and cut-up
3 eggs, slightly beaten
2 teaspoons diced pimiento, drained
¼ teaspoon Worcestershire sauce
  Dash salt
  Dash cayenne

4 servings

In 1-quart casserole, combine butter, green pepper and onion. Cover. Microwave at High for 2 to 3 minutes, or until tender-crisp. Stir in oysters. Re-cover. Reduce power to 70% (Medium High). Microwave for 1½ to 2½ minutes, or just until edges of oysters begin to curl. Drain. Stir in remaining ingredients. Microwave, uncovered, at 70% (Medium High) for 2½ to 4½ minutes, or until almost set, stirring twice. Let stand, covered, for 3 minutes. Serve open-face or as filling between slices of toast.

Combine second portion cream cheese with chicken, almonds and garlic powder. Mix well. Set aside. Stir shrimp and water chestnuts into third portion cream cheese. Mix well. Set aside.

Slice loaf crosswise into 4 equal layers. Spread salmon mixture on bottom layer. Top with bread. Spread chicken mixture on bread. Top with bread. Spread shrimp mixture on bread. Top with last layer of bread.

Cover with plastic wrap. Chill for at least 3 hours before serving. Cut into slices.

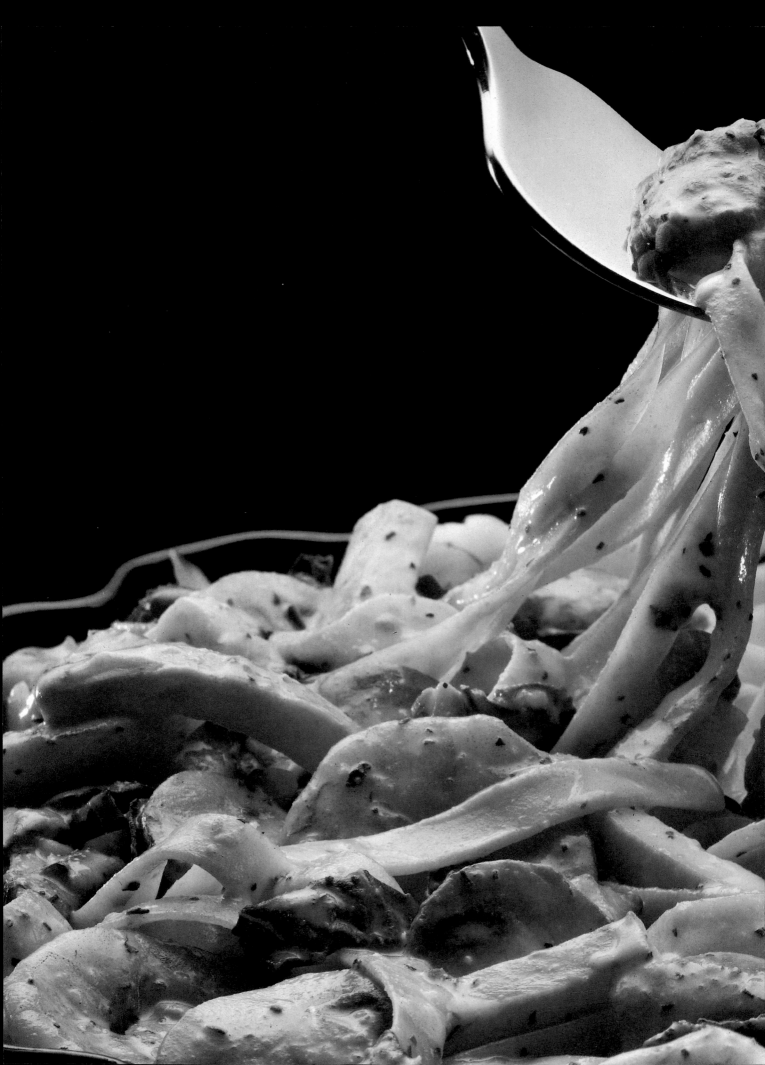

Main Dishes

How to Microwave Stuffed Chicken Italiano

Place butter in medium mixing bowl. Microwave at High for 45 seconds to 1 minute, or until butter melts.

Stir in bread crumbs, cheese, Italian seasoning and cayenne.

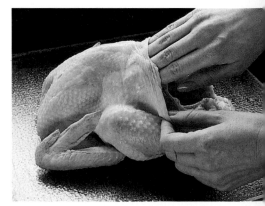

Loosen and lift skin gently from breast of chicken.

Poultry

◄ Stuffed Chicken Italiano

- 3 tablespoons butter or margarine
- ⅔ cup seasoned dry bread crumbs
- 3 tablespoons grated Romano cheese
- ½ teaspoon Italian seasoning
- ⅛ teaspoon cayenne
- 2½ to 3-lb. whole broiler-fryer chicken
- 1 can (16 oz.) whole tomatoes, drained and cut-up
- 1 can (14½ oz.) ready-to-serve chicken broth
- 1 medium onion, cut into 8 pieces
- ⅓ cup white wine
- ½ teaspoon salt

4 servings

Cumin-spiced Chicken

- 2 teaspoons white wine vinegar
- ¾ teaspoon garlic salt
- ½ teaspoon ground cumin
- ¼ teaspoon ground oregano
- ⅛ teaspoon ground allspice
- ⅛ teaspoon pepper
- ¼ teaspoon bouquet sauce
  Dash ground cloves
- 2½ to 3-lb. whole broiler-fryer chicken

4 servings

In small bowl, blend all ingredients, except chicken. Brush or rub spice mixture on chicken. Rub about ½ teaspoon mixture in cavity of chicken. Place chicken breast-side up on roasting rack. Secure legs together with string. Cover with wax paper. Microwave at High for 18 to 25 minutes, or until legs move freely and juices run clear, rotating rack twice. Let stand, covered, for 10 minutes before carving.

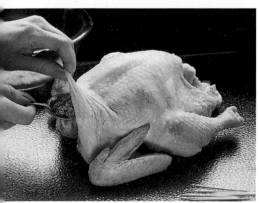

Stuff crumb mixture under skin. Replace skin and secure with wooden pick.

Secure legs together with string. Place chicken breast-side up in deep 3-quart casserole. Add remaining ingredients. Cover.

Microwave at High for 20 to 35 minutes, or until legs move freely and juices run clear, basting with broth after every 10 minutes.

91

Orange-glazed Chicken ▲

Orange Glaze:
- ⅓ cup orange marmalade
- 1 tablespoon olive oil
- 2 teaspoons white wine vinegar
- ½ teaspoon dried mint leaves
- ¼ teaspoon dried rosemary leaves, crushed
- ⅛ teaspoon garlic powder
- ¼ teaspoon bouquet sauce

2½ to 3-lb. broiler-fryer chicken, cut into 8 pieces

4 servings

In 2-cup measure, blend all Orange Glaze ingredients. Microwave at 50% (Medium) for 1 to 1½ minutes, or until warm. Stir. Brush on chicken. Arrange chicken on roasting rack with thickest portions toward outside of rack. Cover with wax paper. Microwave at 70% (Medium High) for 15 to 25 minutes, or until chicken near bone is no longer pink and juices run clear, rearranging and brushing with glaze twice. Let stand, covered, for 3 to 5 minutes.

Salsa Chicken

- 1 can (16 oz.) kidney beans, drained
- 1 cup frozen corn
- 2½ to 3-lb. broiler-fryer chicken, cut into 8 pieces, skin removed
- 1 jar (12 oz.) salsa sauce
- 3 tablespoons tomato paste
- 1 teaspoon instant chicken bouillon granules
- ½ teaspoon dried oregano leaves

4 servings

In 10-inch square casserole, combine kidney beans and corn. Arrange chicken over vegetables with thickest portions toward outside of casserole. In small mixing bowl, combine remaining ingredients. Pour over chicken. Cover. Microwave at High for 3 minutes. Reduce power to 70% (Medium High). Microwave for 25 to 32 minutes, or until chicken near bone is no longer pink and juices run clear, rotating casserole 3 times. Let stand, covered, for 5 minutes. Serve over hot cooked rice.

Classic Herb Chicken

2½ to 3-lb. broiler-fryer chicken, cut into 8 pieces, skin removed

Marinade:
- ⅓ cup white wine
- 3 tablespoons olive oil
- ¾ teaspoon salt
- ¾ teaspoon bouquet garni seasoning
- 1 clove garlic, minced
- ¼ teaspoon sugar
- ¼ teaspoon dried tarragon leaves
- ⅛ teaspoon dry mustard
  Dash pepper

4 servings

Place chicken pieces in large plastic food storage bag in baking dish. Set aside. In 1-cup measure, blend all marinade ingredients. Pour over chicken. Secure bag. Marinate in refrigerator for at least 6 hours.

Remove chicken from marinade. Arrange chicken on roasting rack with thickest portions toward outside of rack. Cover with wax paper. Microwave at High for 13 to 19 minutes, or until chicken near bone is no longer pink and juices run clear, rotating rack once or twice.

Chicken & Shrimp with Couscous

- 1 tablespoon vegetable oil
- ½ cup chopped red pepper
- ½ cup chopped green pepper
- 1 medium onion, chopped
- 1 can (16 oz.) whole tomatoes
- ¾ cup ready-to-serve chicken broth
- 1 teaspoon paprika
- ¾ teaspoon salt
- ¼ teaspoon dried thyme leaves
  Dash cayenne
- 1 pkg. (10 oz.) frozen asparagus cuts
- 2½ to 3-lb. broiler-fryer chicken, cut into 8 pieces, skin removed
- 1⅓ cups uncooked couscous
- ½ lb. small shrimp, shelled and deveined

8 servings

In 3-quart casserole, combine oil, red and green peppers and onion. Cover. Microwave at High for 4 to 6 minutes, or until tender-crisp, stirring once. Add tomatoes, broth, paprika, salt, thyme and cayenne, stirring to break apart tomatoes. Add asparagus. Arrange chicken over vegetables with thickest portions toward outside of casserole. Re-cover. Microwave at High for 22 to 30 minutes, or until chicken near bone is no longer pink and juices run clear, rearranging chicken and stirring 3 times to break apart vegetables. Place chicken in medium bowl. Cover. Set aside.

Stir couscous into hot broth and vegetables. Arrange shrimp over vegetables. Re-cover. Reduce power to 50% (Medium). Microwave for 4 to 7 minutes, or until shrimp are opaque, rearranging shrimp once. Spoon shrimp and couscous mixture onto serving platter. Serve chicken with couscous.

Chicken & Broccoli with Tangy Cream Sauce

2 pkgs. (10 oz. each) frozen broccoli spears
2 medium carrots, cut into 2 × ¼-inch strips, about 1 cup
2 bone-in chicken breasts (10 to 12 oz. each) split in half, skin removed

Sauce:
¼ cup butter or margarine
2 tablespoons all-purpose flour
½ teaspoon salt
½ teaspoon grated lemon peel
⅛ teaspoon cayenne
1⅓ cups milk
2 egg yolks, slightly beaten
2 teaspoons lemon juice
Paprika

4 servings

Unwrap broccoli and place in 9-inch square baking dish. Microwave at High for 4½ to 5½ minutes, or until defrosted, breaking apart after half the time. Drain. Arrange broccoli with flowerets toward center of same baking dish. Arrange carrots evenly over broccoli. Place chicken breast halves over vegetables. Cover with plastic wrap. Microwave at High for 9 to 13½ minutes, or until chicken is no longer pink, rearranging chicken after half the time. Drain. Let stand, covered, while preparing sauce.

Place butter in 4-cup measure. Microwave at High for 1 to 1½ minutes, or until butter melts. Stir in flour, salt, lemon peel and cayenne. Blend in milk. Microwave at High for 3½ to 5 minutes, or until mixture thickens slightly and just begins to boil, stirring 2 or 3 times. Blend small amount of hot mixture into egg yolks. Add back to hot mixture, stirring constantly. Reduce power to 50% (Medium). Microwave for 1 to 1½ minutes, or until mixture thickens, stirring after every 30 seconds. Blend in lemon juice. Pour sauce over chicken. Sprinkle with paprika.

Creamy Dijon Chicken

1 pkg. (9 oz.) frozen artichoke hearts
2 bone-in chicken breasts (10 to 12 oz. each) split in half, skin removed
⅓ cup sliced black olives

Sauce:

2 tablespoons butter or margarine
3 tablespoons all-purpose flour
¾ teaspoon salt
½ teaspoon onion powder
½ teaspoon dried parsley flakes
   Dash pepper
1 tablespoon Dijon mustard
½ cup ready-to-serve chicken broth
1 cup half-and-half

4 servings

Unwrap artichoke hearts and place on plate. Microwave at High for 4 to 5 minutes, or until defrosted. Drain. Place in 9-inch square baking dish. Arrange chicken over artichoke hearts. Top with olives. Set aside.

Place butter in 4-cup measure. Microwave at High for 45 seconds to 1 minute, or until butter melts. Stir in flour, salt, onion powder, parsley, pepper and Dijon mustard. Blend in broth and half-and-half. Reduce power to 70% (Medium High). Microwave for 5½ to 8½ minutes, or until mixture thickens and bubbles, stirring 2 or 3 times. Pour over chicken. Cover with wax paper. Microwave at 70% (Medium High) for 20 to 29 minutes, or until chicken is no longer pink, rearranging chicken once or twice. Let stand, covered, for 3 to 4 minutes.

Chicken Breasts ▶ Veronique

4 boneless whole chicken
  breasts (8 to 10 oz. each)
  skin removed

Stuffing:
2 tablespoons butter or
  margarine
⅓ cup chopped fresh
  mushrooms
1 tablespoon finely chopped
  onion
⅓ cup sliced seedless green
  grapes
¼ cup unseasoned dry bread
  crumbs
2 tablespoons raisins
¼ teaspoon celery salt
¼ teaspoon ground coriander

Sauce:
1 can (10¾ oz.) condensed
  cream of mushroom soup
2 tablespoons milk
½ teaspoon dried parsley
  flakes
⅛ teaspoon pepper

4 servings

Pound each chicken breast
between two sheets of plastic
wrap to ¼-inch thickness. Set
aside. In small mixing bowl,
combine butter, mushrooms and
onion. Cover with plastic wrap.
Microwave at High for 2 minutes.
Stir in remaining stuffing ingredients. Spread one-fourth of
stuffing on each chicken breast
to within ½ inch of edges. Fold
in sides and roll up, enclosing
stuffing. Secure with wooden
picks. Arrange seam-side down
in 9-inch square baking dish. In
small mixing bowl, combine all
sauce ingredients. Pour over
chicken breasts. Cover with wax
paper. Microwave at 70%
(Medium High) for 16 to 24 minutes, or until chicken is firm and
no longer pink, rearranging
chicken once or twice. Let
stand, covered, for 3 to 5
minutes. Remove wooden picks.

Spinach & Scallop-stuffed Chicken Breasts ▲

4 boneless whole chicken
  breasts (8 to 10 oz. each)
  skin removed
1 tablespoon butter or
  margarine
2 tablespoons chopped onion
¼ teaspoon garlic powder
¼ teaspoon dried thyme leaves
1 pkg. (10 oz.) frozen chopped
  spinach
¼ lb. bay scallops, cut in half

½ cup shredded Swiss cheese
¼ teaspoon salt

Coating:
½ cup cornflake crumbs
1 tablespoon dried parsley
  flakes
1 teaspoon paprika
⅛ teaspoon garlic powder

2 tablespoons butter or
  margarine

4 servings

Pound each chicken breast between two sheets of plastic wrap to
⅛-inch thickness. Set aside. In 1-quart casserole, combine butter,
onion, garlic powder and thyme. Cover. Microwave at High for
1½ to 2½ minutes, or until onion is tender, stirring after half the
time. Set aside.

Unwrap spinach and place on plate. Microwave at High for 4 to
5 minutes, or until defrosted. Drain thoroughly, pressing to remove
excess moisture. Add to onion mixture. Stir in scallops, cheese and
salt. Spread one-fourth of spinach mixture down center of each
chicken breast. Fold in sides and roll up, enclosing filling. Secure
with wooden picks. Set aside.

On wax paper, combine all coating ingredients. Set aside. Place
butter in 9-inch pie plate. Microwave at High for 45 seconds to
1 minute, or until butter melts. Dip each stuffed breast in melted
butter, then roll in coating mixture, pressing lightly. Place seam-side
down on roasting rack. Microwave at 70% (Medium High) for 13 to
15 minutes, or until chicken is firm and no longer pink, rotating rack
after every 5 minutes. Remove wooden picks.

Chicken Pasta Supreme

⅓ cup butter or margarine
1 clove garlic, minced
1 cup julienne yellow squash
   (2 × ¼-inch strips)
1 cup fresh cauliflowerets
½ cup thinly sliced red onion
2 tablespoons snipped fresh
   parsley
½ teaspoon salt
¼ teaspoon pepper
¼ teaspoon ground nutmeg
1 boneless whole chicken
   breast (8 to 10 oz.) skin
   removed, cut into 1-inch
   cubes
⅓ cup half-and-half
¼ cup grated Parmesan
   cheese
8 oz. fettuccine, cooked
2 tablespoons sliced almonds

4 servings

In 2-quart casserole, combine
butter and garlic. Microwave at
High for 1 to 3 minutes, or until
butter melts. Stir in squash,
cauliflower, onion, parsley, salt,
pepper, nutmeg and chicken.
Cover with wax paper. Microwave at High for 4 to 7 minutes,
or until chicken is no longer
pink and vegetables are tender-
crisp, stirring after every 2
minutes. Add half-and-half
and Parmesan cheese. Stir.
Serve over hot fettuccine.
Sprinkle with almonds.

Saucy Chicken & Summer Vegetables ▲

2 tablespoons butter or
   margarine
2 cups julienne carrots
   (1½ × ¼-inch strips)
2 cups julienne zucchini
   (1½ × ¼-inch strips)
2 boneless whole chicken
   breasts (8 to 10 oz. each)
   split in half, skin removed

1 can (10¾ oz.) condensed
   cream of onion soup
2 tablespoons milk
½ teaspoon seasoned salt
¼ teaspoon dried basil leaves
¼ teaspoon dried summer
   savory leaves
   Dash pepper

4 servings

In 9-inch square baking dish, combine butter, carrots and zucchini.
Cover with plastic wrap. Microwave at High for 4 to 6 minutes, or
until zucchini is tender-crisp, stirring once. Arrange chicken over
vegetables. In small mixing bowl, combine remaining ingredients.
Pour evenly over chicken. Cover with wax paper. Reduce power
to 70% (Medium High). Microwave for 13 to 20 minutes, or until
chicken is no longer pink, rearranging chicken and stirring vegetables 2 or 3 times. Let stand, covered, for 5 minutes.

Orange Chicken with Oriental Vegetables

1 boneless whole chicken
   breast (8 to 10 oz.) skin
   removed, cut into ¾-inch
   cubes
1 tablespoon vegetable oil
1 clove garlic, minced
¼ teaspoon grated orange peel
1 can (14 oz.) bean sprouts,
   rinsed and drained
1 can (8 oz.) sliced water
   chestnuts, drained
1 pkg. (6 oz.) frozen pea pods
1 cup diagonally sliced
   carrots, ⅛ inch thick
¼ cup orange marmalade
2 tablespoons soy sauce
1 teaspoon vinegar
1 tablespoon cornstarch
¼ teaspoon salt

4 servings

In 2-quart casserole, combine chicken, oil, garlic and orange peel. Cover. Microwave at High for 3 to 5 minutes, or until chicken is no longer pink, stirring after half the time. Remove chicken from casserole. Set aside.

Reserve cooking liquid in casserole. Add bean sprouts, water chestnuts, pea pods, carrots, orange marmalade, soy sauce and vinegar. Mix well. Re-cover. Microwave at High for 6 to 11 minutes, or until carrots are tender-crisp, stirring after every 3 minutes. Stir in chicken. Drain cooking liquid into 4-cup measure. Reserve chicken and vegetables. Blend cornstarch and salt into cooking liquid. Microwave at High for 2 to 3 minutes, or until mixture thickens and bubbles, stirring after every minute. Pour over chicken and vegetables. Toss to coat. Serve over hot cooked rice.

Artichoke & Chicken Bake

- 1 boneless whole chicken breast (8 to 10 oz.) skin removed, cut into 1-inch pieces
- 2 tablespoons butter or margarine
- ⅓ cup chopped onion
- ½ teaspoon dried marjoram leaves
- ¼ teaspoon garlic powder
- ⅛ teaspoon pepper
- 1 cup sliced fresh mushrooms
- 1 pkg. (9 oz.) frozen artichoke hearts
- ½ teaspoon salt
- 4 cups hot cooked brown or white rice
- 1 can (10¾ oz.) condensed cream of chicken soup
- 1 cup shredded Cheddar cheese, divided
- ¼ cup sliced green onions

6 servings

Place chicken pieces in 9-inch pie plate. Cover with plastic wrap. Microwave at High for 3 to 5 minutes, or until chicken is no longer pink, stirring after half the time. Set aside. In 2-quart casserole, combine butter, onion, marjoram, garlic powder and pepper. Cover. Microwave at High for 2 minutes. Stir in mushrooms. Re-cover. Microwave at High for 2 to 3 minutes, or until onion is tender. Set aside.

Unwrap artichoke hearts and place on plate. Microwave at High for 4 to 5 minutes, or until defrosted. Drain. Cut into bite-size pieces. Add artichokes, chicken, salt, rice, soup and ½ cup Cheddar cheese to mushroom mixture. Mix well. Microwave at High for 5 minutes. Stir. Top casserole with remaining ½ cup Cheddar cheese and green onions. Cover. Reduce power to 50% (Medium). Microwave for 12 to 23 minutes, or until heated through, rotating casserole after every 5 minutes.

Cashew-coated Chicken

Coating:
- ¼ cup salted cashews, divided
- ¼ cup cornflake crumbs
- ½ teaspoon five spice powder
- ¼ teaspoon salt
  Dash pepper

- 1 tablespoon butter or margarine
- 1 egg, beaten
- 4 chicken legs (about 1 lb.) skin removed

2 servings

Place 2 tablespoons cashews in blender container. Process until fine particles form. Finely chop remaining 2 tablespoons cashews. On wax paper, combine cashews and remaining coating ingredients. Set aside. Place butter in 9-inch pie plate. Microwave at High for 45 seconds to 1 minute, or until butter melts. Blend in egg. Dip chicken legs in egg mixture, then roll in coating mixture, pressing lightly. Arrange chicken on roasting rack with thickest portions toward outside of rack. Microwave at 70% (Medium High) for 7 to 12 minutes, or until chicken near bone is no longer pink and juices run clear, rotating rack once or twice.

Sesame-Ginger Chicken

Marinade:

½ cup ready-to-serve chicken broth
⅓ cup soy sauce
2 tablespoons finely chopped onion
1 clove garlic, minced
1 tablespoon fresh lime juice
1 teaspoon grated lime peel
½ teaspoon sesame oil
¼ teaspoon salt
¼ teaspoon dried crushed red pepper

4 chicken thighs (about 1¼ lbs.) skin removed

Coating:

½ cup finely crushed sesame melba cracker rounds
⅛ teaspoon garlic powder
⅛ teaspoon ground ginger

2 tablespoons butter or margarine
1 egg, beaten

2 to 4 servings

In small mixing bowl, combine all marinade ingredients. Microwave at High for 1½ to 2½ minutes, or just until mixture boils. Cool slightly. Place large plastic food storage bag in baking dish. Add chicken. Pour marinade over chicken. Secure bag. Marinate in refrigerator for at least 6 hours, turning occasionally.

On wax paper, mix all coating ingredients. Set aside. Place butter in 9-inch pie plate. Microwave at High for 45 seconds to 1 minute, or until butter melts. Blend in egg. Drain chicken. Dip chicken thighs in egg mixture, then roll in coating mixture, pressing lightly. Place chicken on roasting rack. Microwave at 70% (Medium High) for 18 to 23 minutes, or until chicken near bone is no longer pink and juices run clear, rotating rack 1 or 2 times.

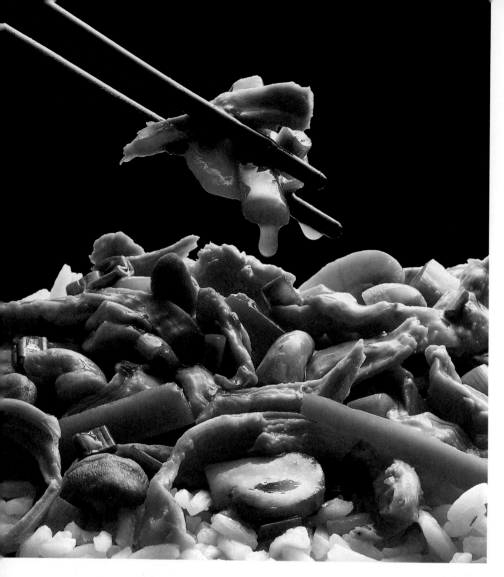

Shredded Chicken & Cashews ▲

⅓ cup ready-to-serve chicken
   broth
1 tablespoon soy sauce
1 tablespoon white wine
1 teaspoon sugar
1 teaspoon cornstarch
½ teaspoon salt
¼ teaspoon dried crushed
   red pepper
¼ teaspoon sesame oil
1 clove garlic, minced

2 cups shredded cooked
   chicken
2 teaspoons vegetable oil
½ cup julienne carrots
   (2 × ¼-inch strips)
½ cup sliced fresh
   mushrooms
½ cup sliced green onions
½ cup sliced water chestnuts
⅓ cup chopped cashews

4 to 6 servings

In medium mixing bowl, combine broth, soy sauce, wine, sugar,
cornstarch, salt, red pepper, sesame oil and garlic. Mix well. Add
chicken. Stir to coat. Set aside. In 2-quart casserole, combine
vegetable oil, carrots, mushrooms, onions and water chestnuts.
Cover. Microwave at High for 4 to 5½ minutes, or until carrots are
just tender-crisp, stirring once. Add chicken mixture and cashews.
Stir. Re-cover. Microwave at High for 3 to 5 minutes, or until very
hot, stirring once. Serve over hot cooked rice.

Mexican
Chicken & Cheese

1 pkg. (3 oz.) cream cheese
½ cup ricotta cheese
½ teaspoon salt
¼ teaspoon ground cumin
⅛ teaspoon ground oregano
⅛ teaspoon pepper
½ cup chopped green pepper
¼ cup chopped onion
1 can (4 oz.) diced green
   chilies, drained
3 cups broken corn chips,
   divided
1 to 1½ cups cut-up cooked
   chicken
1 cup shredded Cheddar
   cheese
1 cup shredded Monterey
   Jack cheese

6 to 8 servings

Place cream cheese in small
mixing bowl. Microwave at High
for 20 to 30 seconds, or until
cheese softens. Stir in ricotta
cheese, salt, cumin, oregano
and pepper. Mix well. Set aside.

In 1-quart casserole, combine
green pepper and onion. Cover.
Microwave at High for 2 to 3
minutes, or until tender-crisp,
stirring once. Mix in chilies.
Set aside.

Sprinkle 2 cups corn chips
evenly over bottom of 9-inch
square baking dish. Sprinkle
chicken evenly over chips. Drop
small spoonfuls of ricotta cheese
mixture onto chicken. Top with
pepper mixture. Microwave at
70% (Medium High) for 5 to
7 minutes, or until hot in center,
rotating dish once. Sprinkle
evenly with Cheddar and
Monterey Jack cheeses. Microwave at 70% (Medium High) for
3 to 5 minutes, or until cheese
melts, rotating dish once. Top
with remaining 1 cup corn
chips. Serve with taco sauce or
dairy sour cream.

Chicken & Broccoli Quiche

Crust:
¾ cup whole wheat flour
½ cup all-purpose flour
½ teaspoon salt
½ teaspoon poultry seasoning
½ cup vegetable shortening
2 to 3 tablespoons cold water

Filling:
1 pkg. (10 oz.) frozen chopped
   broccoli
1 cup cut-up cooked chicken
1 cup shredded Monterey
   Jack cheese
2 tablespoons all-purpose flour
½ teaspoon salt
⅛ teaspoon pepper
½ cup half-and-half
2 eggs, slightly beaten
2 tablespoons butter or
   margarine
½ cup chopped pecans
¼ teaspoon cayenne

6 servings

In small mixing bowl, combine whole wheat and all-purpose flours, salt and poultry seasoning. Cut in shortening to form coarse crumbs. Sprinkle with water, 1 tablespoon at a time, mixing with fork until particles are moistened and cling together. Form dough into a ball. Roll out on lightly floured board at least 2 inches larger than inverted 9-inch pie plate. Ease into pie plate. Trim and flute edges. Prick thoroughly. Microwave at High for 5 to 7½ minutes, or until crust appears dry and opaque, rotating plate after every 2 minutes. Set aside.

For filling, unwrap broccoli and place on plate. Microwave at High for 3 to 4 minutes, or until defrosted. Drain thoroughly, pressing to remove excess moisture. In medium mixing bowl, combine broccoli, chicken, cheese, flour, salt, pepper, half-and-half and eggs. Set aside. In small bowl, combine butter, pecans and cayenne. Microwave at High for 2½ to 3½ minutes, or until pecans begin to brown, stirring after every minute. Drain on paper towels. Pour broccoli and chicken mixture into prepared crust. Sprinkle with pecans. Microwave at 50% (Medium) for 11 to 22 minutes, or until filling is set, rotating plate after every 3 minutes. Let stand for 10 minutes.

Chicken & Ratatouille Potatoes ▲

4 large baking potatoes
  (8 to 9 oz. each)
1 tablespoon olive oil
1 tablespoon sliced green
  onion
1 clove garlic, minced
1 medium zucchini, cut in half
  lengthwise and thinly
  sliced, about 1 cup
1 cup sliced fresh
  mushrooms
¼ cup sliced black olives
1 medium tomato, peeled,
  seeded and chopped

Sauce:

2 tablespoons butter or
  margarine
2 tablespoons all-purpose
  flour
½ teaspoon salt
¼ teaspoon dried thyme
  leaves
1¼ cups milk
⅔ cup shredded Cheddar
  cheese
1 cup cut-up cooked chicken

4 servings

Pierce potatoes with fork. Arrange in circular pattern on paper towel in microwave oven. Microwave at High for 12 to 16 minutes, or until tender. Wrap in foil. Set aside.

In 2-quart casserole, combine olive oil, onion and garlic. Cover. Microwave at High for 1½ to 3 minutes, or until onion is tender. Stir in zucchini, mushrooms and olives. Re-cover. Microwave at High for 3½ to 4 minutes, or until vegetables are tender-crisp. Stir in tomato. Set aside.

For sauce, place butter in 4-cup measure. Microwave at High for 45 seconds to 1 minute, or until butter melts. Stir in flour, salt and thyme. Blend in milk. Microwave at High for 2½ to 5 minutes, or until mixture thickens and bubbles, stirring after every minute. Stir in cheese until melted. Stir in chicken. Cut each potato in half lengthwise. Serve chicken and vegetables over potatoes.

Chicken Livers in Rich Mushroom Sauce

2 tablespoons butter or
  margarine
¾ cup chopped onion
1 tablespoon snipped fresh
  parsley
¼ teaspoon dried rosemary
  leaves
3 tablespoons all-purpose flour
⅛ teaspoon pepper
1 can (10½ oz.) condensed
  beef broth
¼ cup red wine
1 lb. chicken livers, rinsed and
  drained
1 jar (4½ oz.) sliced
  mushrooms, drained

6 servings

In 1½-quart casserole, combine butter, onion, parsley and rosemary. Cover. Microwave at High for 4 to 5 minutes, or until onion is tender, stirring once. Stir in flour and pepper. Blend in broth and wine. Stir in remaining ingredients. Reduce power to 70% (Medium High). Microwave, uncovered, for 16 to 20 minutes, or until chicken livers are no longer pink and mixture has thickened, stirring 3 times. Serve over hot cooked noodles.

Boneless Herb-roasted Turkey

5 to 6-lb. boneless whole
    turkey
3 cloves garlic, each cut into
    4 pieces
1½ teaspoons dried rosemary
    leaves
¾ teaspoon dried marjoram
    leaves
¼ teaspoon pepper

8 to 10 servings

Cut twelve 1-inch slits in turkey. Insert garlic pieces. In small bowl, combine rosemary, marjoram and pepper. Sprinkle evenly over turkey. Place in nylon cooking bag. Secure bag loosely with string. Place in 10-inch square casserole. Microwave at High for 10 minutes. Reduce power to 70% (Medium High). Microwave for 45 minutes to 1¼ hours, or until internal temperature registers 175°F in several places, turning turkey over after every 30 minutes. Let stand, tented with foil, for 15 to 20 minutes before carving.

Herb & Vegetable-stuffed Turkey Tenderloins

1 cup frozen cut green beans
2 tablespoons butter or margarine
¼ cup chopped carrot
¼ cup chopped celery
2 tablespoons finely chopped onion
½ cup herb seasoned stuffing mix
¼ teaspoon salt

Gravy:

1 tablespoon butter or margarine
2 tablespoons all-purpose flour
2 teaspoons dried parsley flakes
¼ teaspoon salt
⅛ teaspoon pepper
¼ teaspoon bouquet sauce
½ cup ready-to-serve chicken broth
¾ cup milk

2 turkey tenderloins (about 1 lb.)
Paprika

4 servings

How to Microwave Herb & Vegetable-stuffed Turkey Tenderloins

Place beans on plate. Microwave at High for 1 to 2½ minutes, or until defrosted. Coarsely chop beans. In 1-quart casserole, combine beans, butter, carrot, celery and onion. Cover.

Microwave at High for 4 to 5 minutes, or until vegetables are tender, stirring after every 2 minutes. Stir in stuffing mix and salt. Re-cover. Set aside. Place butter in 4-cup measure. Microwave at High for 45 seconds to 1 minute, or until butter melts.

Stir in flour, parsley, salt, pepper and bouquet sauce. Blend in broth until smooth. Blend in milk. Microwave at High for 3 to 3½ minutes, or until mixture thickens, stirring after every minute.

Cut lengthwise slit in each tenderloin to within ½ inch of edge to form pocket. Fill each tenderloin with half of stuffing mixture.

Arrange in 9-inch square baking dish with stuffing opening toward center of dish. Pour gravy over turkey. Sprinkle with paprika. Cover with wax paper.

Microwave at 70% (Medium High) for 13 to 18 minutes, or until turkey is firm and no longer pink, rotating dish after every 3 minutes.

Ham-stuffed Turkey Tenderloins ▲

2 turkey tenderloins
  (about 1¼ lbs.)

Stuffing:
1 tablespoon butter or
  margarine
2 tablespoons chopped onion
1 tablespoon finely chopped
  celery
1 tablespoon finely chopped
  red or green pepper
¼ lb. ground fully cooked ham
⅓ cup fresh bread crumbs
1 teaspoon dried parsley
  flakes

1 tablespoon milk
¼ teaspoon dried crushed
  sage leaves
  Dash salt
  Dash pepper

Basting Sauce:
1 tablespoon butter or
  margarine
1 teaspoon dried parsley
  flakes
⅛ teaspoon dried crushed
  sage leaves

4 to 6 servings

Cut lengthwise slit in each turkey tenderloin to within ½ inch of edge to form pocket for stuffing. Set aside. In 1-quart casserole, combine butter, onion, celery and red pepper. Cover. Microwave at High for 2 to 3 minutes, or until celery is tender-crisp. Stir in remaining stuffing ingredients. Fill each tenderloin with half of stuffing. Secure with string in 2 or 3 places. Arrange in 9-inch square baking dish with stuffing opening toward center of dish. Set aside. In custard cup, combine all basting sauce ingredients. Microwave at High for 45 seconds to 1 minute, or until butter melts. Brush on each tenderloin. Cover with wax paper. Microwave at 70% (Medium High) for 11 to 18 minutes, or until turkey is firm and no longer pink, rotating dish twice. Let stand, covered, for 3 minutes. Remove string.

Barbecued Turkey Thighs

2 turkey thighs (1 to 1½ lbs.
  each)
1 can (8 oz.) tomato sauce
1 tablespoon honey
2 teaspoons cider vinegar
2 teaspoons Worcestershire
  sauce
½ teaspoon prepared mustard
¼ teaspoon salt
⅛ teaspoon celery seed
⅛ teaspoon pepper
⅛ teaspoon instant minced
  garlic

4 servings

Arrange turkey thighs in 10-inch square casserole with thickest portions toward outside of casserole. Set aside. In small mixing bowl, combine remaining ingredients. Mix well. Pour over turkey. Cover. Marinate in refrigerator for at least 4 hours.

Place casserole with turkey and marinade in microwave oven. Microwave at High for 5 minutes. Reduce power to 70% (Medium High). Microwave for 30 to 40 minutes, or until turkey is tender and cooked through, turning turkey over and basting with sauce twice. Remove turkey from bones and serve in sauce.

108

Apple-Plum Spiced Turkey Breast

5¼ to 6¼-lb. bone-in turkey
   breast, defrosted

Marinade:

½ cup apple juice
⅓ cup plum jelly
⅓ cup Hoisen sauce
 1 tablespoon soy sauce
¼ teaspoon fennel seed,
   crushed
¼ teaspoon ground cinnamon
⅛ teaspoon anise seed,
   crushed
⅛ teaspoon ground cloves

6 to 8 servings

Remove gravy packet from turkey breast and discard. Place turkey in large plastic food storage bag in baking dish. In 4-cup measure, combine all marinade ingredients. Microwave at High for 2½ to 3½ minutes, or until mixture boils, stirring after every minute. Cool slightly. Pour over turkey. Secure bag. Marinate in refrigerator overnight, turning bag occasionally.

Remove turkey breast from marinade, reserving marinade. Place turkey skin-side down on roasting rack. Estimate total cooking time at 12½ to 16½ minutes per pound and divide total cooking time into 4 parts. Microwave at High for first 5 minutes. Reduce power to 50% (Medium). Microwave the remainder of first one-fourth of time. Turn turkey on side. Brush with marinade. Microwave at 50% (Medium) for second one-fourth of time. Turn turkey on other side. Brush with marinade. Microwave at 50% (Medium) for third one-fourth of time. Turn turkey skin-side up. Brush with marinade. Microwave the remaining one-fourth of time, or until internal temperature registers 170°F in several places. Let stand, tented with foil, for 10 to 20 minutes before carving.

Hungarian Turkey Goulash

 1 teaspoon vegetable oil
 1 medium onion, cut in half
   lengthwise and thinly
   sliced
 1 clove garlic, minced
 1 tablespoon all-purpose flour
 1 can (8 oz.) whole tomatoes
⅓ cup water
 2 teaspoons paprika
1½ teaspoons instant beef
   bouillon granules
½ teaspoon salt
¼ teaspoon caraway seed,
   crushed
 2 medium potatoes, thinly
   sliced, about 2 cups
1½ cups cubed turkey, ¾-inch
   cubes
⅓ cup dairy sour cream

4 servings

In 1½-quart casserole, combine oil, onion and garlic. Cover. Microwave at High for 4 to 6 minutes, or until onion is tender, stirring once. Stir in flour. Mix in tomatoes and water, stirring to break apart tomatoes. Stir in paprika, bouillon, salt, caraway, potatoes and turkey. Re-cover. Microwave at High for 15 to 20 minutes, or until potatoes are tender, stirring 3 times. Let stand, covered, for 5 minutes. Stir in sour cream.

Cutlets with Cheese ▲

⅓ cup mayonnaise
⅓ cup dairy sour cream
 1 tablespoon Dijon mustard
½ teaspoon Worcestershire
   sauce
⅛ teaspoon cayenne
 4 turkey cutlets (2 to 3 oz.
   each) ¼ inch thick
 2 cups garlic and onion
   seasoned croutons,
   crushed
 4 slices (½ oz. each) Cheddar
   cheese, cut into
   3 × 1½-inch strips

4 servings

In 9-inch square baking dish, combine mayonnaise, sour cream, mustard, Worcestershire sauce and cayenne. Mix well. Add turkey cutlets, turning to coat. Cover. Chill for 1 to 2 hours. Scrape excess sour cream mixture from cutlets. Dip each cutlet in crumbs, pressing lightly to coat both sides. Arrange cutlets on roasting rack. Microwave at 70% (Medium High) for 3 minutes. Rotate rack half turn. Top each cutlet with Cheddar cheese. Microwave at 70% (Medium High) for 5 to 6 minutes, or until cheese melts and turkey is firm and no longer pink, rotating rack after half the time.

109

Turkey Cutlets & Golden Pilaf

Golden Pilaf:

- 1 slice bacon, cut-up
- 2 tablespoons sliced green onion
- 1½ cups ready-to-serve chicken broth
- ½ cup chopped red apple
- ⅓ cup raisins
- ½ teaspoon dried parsley flakes
- ¼ teaspoon salt
- ¼ teaspoon turmeric
- ¼ teaspoon lemon pepper seasoning
- 1½ cups instant rice

- ½ cup cornflake crumbs
- 1 teaspoon dried parsley flakes
- ½ teaspoon lemon pepper seasoning
- 12 oz. turkey cutlets (2 to 3 oz. each) ¼ inch thick
- 2 tablespoons chopped walnuts

4 servings

In 2-quart casserole, combine bacon and onion. Cover. Microwave at High for 2 to 4 minutes, or until bacon is brown. Stir in remaining pilaf ingredients, except rice. Re-cover. Microwave at High for 5 to 8 minutes, or until mixture boils. Quickly stir in rice. Re-cover. Set aside.

On wax paper, combine cornflake crumbs, parsley and lemon pepper. Roll each cutlet in crumb mixture, pressing lightly to coat. Arrange cutlets on roasting rack. Cover with wax paper. Microwave at 70% (Medium High) for 5 to 11 minutes, or until turkey is firm and no longer pink, rotating rack once. Add walnuts to pilaf. Stir. Spoon pilaf onto serving platter. Serve cutlets with pilaf.

Turkey Tamale Pie

Topping:
½ cup dairy sour cream
⅛ teaspoon ground cumin
⅛ teaspoon ground coriander
    Dash salt

Crust:
1 cup all-purpose flour
⅓ cup yellow cornmeal
¾ teaspoon salt
¼ teaspoon chili powder
    Dash cayenne
6 tablespoons shortening
4 to 6 tablespoons cold water

Filling:
1 lb. ground turkey
⅓ cup chopped green pepper
1 clove garlic, minced
1 teaspoon chili powder
¼ teaspoon salt
⅛ teaspoon ground cumin
⅛ teaspoon ground coriander
⅛ teaspoon ground oregano
    Dash cayenne
2 cups shredded Cheddar
    cheese
¼ cup chili sauce

6 servings

In small mixing bowl, combine all topping ingredients. Chill topping while preparing crust and filling.

For crust, in small mixing bowl, combine flour, cornmeal, salt, chili powder and cayenne. Cut in shortening to form coarse crumbs. Sprinkle with water, 1 tablespoon at a time, mixing with fork until particles are moistened and cling together. Form dough into a ball. Roll out on lightly floured board at least 2 inches larger than inverted 9-inch pie plate. Ease into plate. Trim and flute edges. Prick thoroughly. Microwave at High for 6 to 9 minutes, or until crust appears dry and opaque, rotating plate after every 2 minutes. Set aside.

In 2-quart casserole, combine all filling ingredients, except cheese and chili sauce. Microwave at High for 4 to 6 minutes, or until turkey is firm and cooked through, stirring after every 2 minutes. Drain. Stir in cheese and chili sauce. Press mixture into prepared crust. Spread topping over filling to within 1 inch of edge. Microwave at 50% (Medium) for 8 to 14 minutes, or until heated through, rotating plate after every 3 minutes. Serve with chopped tomato and sliced green onion.

111

Greek Pasticchio ▲

1 lb. ground turkey
⅓ cup chopped onion
¾ teaspoon ground cinnamon
⅛ teaspoon ground nutmeg
⅔ cup ricotta cheese
½ teaspoon dried parsley flakes
¼ teaspoon salt
⅛ teaspoon pepper

Sauce:
2 tablespoons butter or margarine
2 tablespoons all-purpose flour
½ teaspoon salt
1¼ cups milk
¼ cup grated Parmesan cheese

1⅓ cups fine egg noodles, cooked
Snipped fresh parsley (optional)

4 to 6 servings

In 1½-quart casserole, combine turkey and onion. Microwave at High for 4 to 7 minutes, or until firm, stirring twice. Drain. Stir in cinnamon and nutmeg. Microwave at High for 1 minute. Place turkey mixture in medium bowl. Set aside. In small mixing bowl, blend ricotta cheese, parsley, salt and pepper. Set aside.

For sauce, place butter in small mixing bowl. Microwave at High for 45 seconds to 1 minute, or until butter melts. Stir in flour and salt. Blend in milk. Microwave at High for 4 to 6½ minutes, or until mixture thickens and bubbles, stirring 2 or 3 times with whisk. Blend in Parmesan cheese. In same 1½-quart casserole, layer half of noodles, half of turkey, half of ricotta cheese mixture and one-third of sauce. Repeat once, ending with remaining two-thirds of sauce. Microwave at High for 5 minutes. Rotate casserole half turn. Reduce power to 50% (Medium). Microwave for 6 to 12 minutes, or until heated through, rotating casserole twice. Let stand for 3 minutes. Garnish with snipped fresh parsley.

Burrito Bake ▶

¾ lb. ground turkey
6 oz. pork sausage
⅓ cup chopped onion
1 teaspoon ground cumin
½ teaspoon salt
¼ teaspoon garlic powder
¼ teaspoon dried crushed red pepper
¼ teaspoon pepper
1¼ cups taco or salsa sauce, divided
¼ cup chopped black olives
⅔ cup refried beans
4 flour tortillas, 10-inch
1 cup shredded Monterey Jack cheese
½ cup shredded Cheddar cheese

Toppings:
Sliced avocado
Shredded lettuce
Chopped tomato
Dairy sour cream

4 servings

In 2-quart casserole, combine turkey, sausage and onion. Microwave at High for 6 to 8 minutes or until meats are firm, stirring 2 or 3 times. Drain. Add cumin, salt, garlic powder, red pepper, pepper, ½ cup taco sauce and olives. Mix well. Stir in refried beans. Microwave at High for 3 minutes, stirring once. Set aside.

Prepare tortillas as directed on package for enchiladas. Spoon one-fourth of turkey mixture down center of each tortilla. Fold in one end of tortilla and then two sides. Roll to enclose filling. Place burritos seam-side down in 10-inch square casserole. Top with remaining ¾ cup taco sauce. Sprinkle with Monterey Jack and Cheddar cheeses. Microwave at 70% (Medium High) for 6 to 9 minutes, or until cheese melts and burritos are hot, rotating once or twice. Let stand, covered, for 3 minutes. Serve with toppings.

Layered Turkey Florentine Loaf ▼

Turkey Layer:
- 1 lb. ground turkey
- 1 egg
- ¼ cup seasoned dry bread crumbs
- 2 tablespoons finely chopped onion
- 2 tablespoons milk
- ½ teaspoon salt
- ⅛ teaspoon pepper

Florentine Layer:
- 1 pkg. (10 oz.) frozen chopped spinach
- 1 cup ricotta cheese
- ¼ cup grated Parmesan cheese
- 1 egg
- ½ teaspoon Italian seasoning
- ¼ teaspoon salt
- ⅛ teaspoon pepper

Topping:
- 1 can (8 oz.) whole tomatoes, drained, cut-up
- ⅓ cup spaghetti sauce

6 servings

In medium mixing bowl, combine all turkey layer ingredients. Mix well. Set aside. Unwrap spinach and place on plate. Microwave at High for 4 to 5 minutes, or until defrosted. Drain thoroughly, pressing to remove excess moisture. In small mixing bowl, combine spinach and remaining Florentine layer ingredients. Mix well. Set aside.

Press half of turkey mixture into 8 × 4-inch loaf dish. Spread Florentine layer over turkey. Spread evenly with remaining turkey mixture. Cover with wax paper. Place on saucer in microwave oven. Microwave at High for 5 minutes. Rotate dish half turn. Reduce power to 70% (Medium High). Microwave for 15 to 23 minutes, or until center bottom of loaf appears cooked and internal temperature in center registers 150°F, rotating dish once or twice. In 2-cup measure, combine topping ingredients. Spread topping over loaf. Reduce power to 50% (Medium). Microwave for 2 minutes to heat through. Let stand for 5 minutes.

Turkey & Bacon Patties ▶

Turkey Mixture:
- 1 lb. ground turkey
- 1 egg
- 3 tablespoons seasoned dry bread crumbs
- 3 tablespoons milk
- 2 tablespoons finely chopped onion
- ½ teaspoon salt
- ¼ teaspoon dried crushed sage leaves
- ⅛ teaspoon pepper

Topping:
- 2 teaspoons butter or margarine
- ¼ cup finely chopped fresh mushrooms
- ¼ cup finely chopped zucchini
- 3 tablespoons seasoned dry bread crumbs
- Dash salt
- Dash pepper

- 4 slices bacon
- Paprika

4 servings

In medium mixing bowl, combine all turkey mixture ingredients. Mix well. Set aside. In 1-quart casserole, combine butter, mushrooms and zucchini. Cover. Microwave at High for 2 to 3 minutes, or until tender. Stir in remaining topping ingredients. Shape turkey mixture into 4 patties, about 1 inch thick. Press in center of each patty to make slight hollow. Fill with topping, pressing down lightly. Set aside.

Arrange bacon on roasting rack. Microwave at High for 1½ to 2½ minutes, or until partially cooked, but not crisp, rotating rack once. Top each patty with bacon slice, tucking ends under patty. Arrange patties on roasting rack. Microwave at High for 6 to 9 minutes, or until patties are firm and cooked through, rotating rack after every 3 minutes. Sprinkle with paprika.

◄ Cornish Hen Friccasee

- 2 tablespoons butter or margarine
- ½ cup chopped onion
- ½ cup thinly sliced celery
- ¼ cup thinly sliced carrot
- 1 cup fresh mushroom halves
- ⅓ cup water
- ¼ cup rosé wine
- 1 teaspoon instant chicken bouillon granules
- ½ teaspoon salt
- ¼ teaspoon dried basil leaves
- ⅛ teaspoon dried thyme leaves
- ⅛ teaspoon pepper
- 2 Cornish hens (18 oz. each) split in half through breastbone
- 2 tablespoons all-purpose flour
- ¼ cup half-and-half
- ¼ teaspoon bouquet sauce

2 servings

In 10-inch square casserole, combine butter, onion, celery and carrot. Cover. Microwave at High for 6 to 8 minutes, or until tender, stirring twice. Stir in mushrooms, water, wine, bouillon, salt, basil, thyme and pepper. Arrange Cornish hens skin-side up on vegetables. Re-cover. Reduce power to 70% (Medium High). Microwave for 16 to 24 minutes, or until Cornish hens are no longer pink and juices run clear, rearranging hens twice. Drain cooking liquid into 4-cup measure. Set aside. Cover Cornish hens and vegetables. Set aside.

In small mixing bowl, blend flour and half-and-half until smooth. Blend in hot cooking liquid and bouquet sauce. Microwave at High for 3 to 4 minutes, or until mixture thickens and bubbles, stirring after every minute. Pour sauce over Cornish hens and vegetables.

Cheesy Crab-stuffed Cornish Hens

Stuffing:
- 2 slices bacon, cut-up
- 1 can (6 oz.) crab meat, rinsed, drained and cartilage removed
- ½ cup Cheddar cheese croutons
- ¼ cup finely shredded Cheddar cheese
- 1 tablespoon sliced green onion
- ⅛ teaspoon salt
- ⅛ teaspoon pepper
- 2 Cornish hens, (18 oz. each*)

Glaze:
- 1 tablespoon French dressing
- ½ teaspoon bouquet sauce

2 servings

Place bacon in 1-quart casserole. Cover. Microwave at High for 2½ to 4 minutes, or until crisp, stirring once. Stir in remaining stuffing ingredients. Fill cavity of Cornish hens with stuffing. Secure legs together with string. In custard cup, blend all glaze ingredients. Brush glaze on Cornish hens. Arrange hens breast-side up on roasting rack. Microwave at High for 12 to 17 minutes, or until legs move freely and juices run clear, rearranging hens and brushing with glaze once or twice. Let stand, tented with foil, for 5 minutes.

*For Cornish hens weighing 24 oz. each, microwave at High for 17 to 20 minutes.

Crisp-roasted Duckling ▲

- 4 to 5-lb. duckling
- 1 small onion, cut into 8 pieces
- 2 slices lemon

2 to 3 servings

Place duckling breast-side down on roasting rack. Secure neck skin to back with wooden picks. Cover with wax paper. Estimate total cooking time at 6½ to 9½ minutes per pound. Microwave at High for 10 minutes. Drain. Fill cavity with onion and lemon. Return duckling breast-side down on roasting rack. Re-cover. Reduce power to 50% (Medium). Microwave the remainder of first half of total cooking time. Drain. Turn duckling breast-side up. Re-cover. Microwave at 50% (Medium) for second half of time, or until legs move freely and juices run clear. Meanwhile, preheat conventional oven to 400°F. Place duckling in conventional roasting pan. Bake until skin on duckling is crisp and brown, 15 to 20 minutes.

Fish & Shellfish

◄ Trout with Walnut Stuffing

Stuffing:
- 2 tablespoons butter or margarine
- 2 tablespoons finely chopped celery
- 2 tablespoons sliced green onion
- 1 tablespoon snipped fresh parsley
- 1 cup herb seasoned croutons
- ¼ cup chopped walnuts
- 3 tablespoons ready-to-serve chicken broth or water
- ¼ teaspoon salt
- ¼ teaspoon lemon pepper seasoning
- ⅛ teaspoon dried marjoram leaves

- 2 whole trout (6 to 8 oz. each) heads removed

2 servings

In 1-quart casserole, combine butter, celery, onion and parsley. Cover. Microwave at High for 2 to 3 minutes, or until tender-crisp. Add remaining stuffing ingredients. Mix well. Fill each trout with half of stuffing. Arrange trout in 10-inch square casserole with backbones toward outside of casserole. Cover with wax paper. Microwave at 70% (Medium High) for 9 to 14 minutes, or until fish flakes easily with fork near backbone. Let stand, covered, for 2 to 3 minutes.

Poached Trout with Onions & Capers

- 1 bottle (8 oz.) clam juice
- 3 tablespoons fresh lemon juice
- 1 small onion, thinly sliced, separated into rings
- ½ teaspoon salt
- ¼ teaspoon pepper
- 2 whole trout (6 to 8 oz. each) heads removed
- ½ cup seasoned croutons, crushed
- 2 tablespoons butter or margarine
- 1 tablespoon capers, drained
- ⅛ teaspoon dried thyme leaves
- Dash garlic powder

2 servings

In 10-inch square casserole, combine clam juice, lemon juice, onion, salt and pepper. Cover. Microwave at High for 6 to 9 minutes, or just until mixture boils. Arrange trout in casserole with backbones toward outside of casserole. Re-cover. Reduce power to 70% (Medium High). Microwave for 6 to 9 minutes, or until fish flakes easily with fork near backbone, turning fish over after half the time. Place trout on serving platter. Top each trout with onion and croutons. Set aside. In 1-cup measure, combine butter, capers, thyme and garlic powder. Microwave at High for 1 to 1½ minutes, or until butter melts. Spoon evenly over trout.

Salmon with Red Wine Sauce

- 4 salmon steaks (7 to 9 oz. each) 1½ inches thick

Red Wine Sauce:
- 3 tablespoons butter or margarine
- 2 tablespoons red wine
- ½ teaspoon onion powder
- ½ teaspoon dried chervil leaves
- ¼ teaspoon celery salt
- ⅛ teaspoon paprika
- ⅛ teaspoon pepper

4 servings

Arrange salmon steaks in 9-inch square baking dish with thickest portions toward outside of dish. Set aside. In 1-cup measure, combine all Red Wine Sauce ingredients. Microwave at 70% (Medium High) for 1½ to 2½ minutes, or until butter melts. Brush half of sauce on salmon. Cover with wax paper. Microwave at 70% (Medium High) for 14 to 19 minutes, or until fish flakes easily with fork, rotating dish and brushing with sauce twice. Let stand, covered, for 3 minutes.

Salmon with Fruited Almond Butter

¼ cup butter or margarine
⅓ cup slivered almonds
½ teaspoon dried marjoram leaves
½ teaspoon grated orange peel
¼ teaspoon garlic powder
1 small red baking apple, cored and thinly sliced
1 small pear, cored and thinly sliced
2 tablespoons apple jelly
4 salmon steaks (4 oz. each) about ¾ inch thick

4 servings

In 1-quart casserole, combine butter, almonds, marjoram, orange peel and garlic powder. Microwave at High for 3½ to 4½ minutes, or until almonds are brown, stirring after every minute. Drain and reserve butter from almonds. In same casserole, combine almonds, apple slices, pear slices and jelly. Stir. Cover. Microwave at High for 4 to 5 minutes, or until fruit is tender, stirring after half the time. Set aside.

Arrange salmon steaks on roasting rack with thickest portions toward outside of rack. Brush with reserved butter. Microwave at 70% (Medium High) for 6 to 7 minutes, or until fish flakes easily with fork, rotating rack after every 2 to 3 minutes. For each serving, spoon fruit mixture over salmon.

Marinated Halibut Steaks ▲

1 can (8 oz.) whole tomatoes
½ cup green pepper strips
½ cup red pepper strips
1 small onion, thinly sliced
¼ cup steak sauce
1 tablespoon packed brown
   sugar
1 tablespoon olive oil
1 tablespoon vinegar
½ teaspoon chili powder
⅛ teaspoon garlic powder
⅛ teaspoon ground cloves
⅛ teaspoon cayenne
12 oz. halibut steaks, about
   ¾ inch thick, cut into 4
   serving-size pieces

4 servings

In 2-quart casserole, combine all ingredients, except halibut. Mix well. Cover. Microwave at High for 5½ to 6½ minutes, or until vegetables are tender-crisp, stirring after half the time. Cool slightly. Add halibut steaks, turning to coat with marinade. Re-cover. Marinate in refrigerator for 4 hours. Microwave at 50% (Medium) for 8 to 13 minutes, or until fish flakes easily with fork, turning fish over after half the time. Serve with vegetables.

Cod in Sour Cream Sauce

Sauce:
2 tablespoons butter or
   margarine
2 tablespoons all-purpose flour
¼ teaspoon salt
¼ teaspoon lemon pepper
   seasoning
   Dash ground nutmeg
1 cup milk
¼ cup dairy sour cream

1 lb. cod fillets, ¾ to 1 inch
   thick, cut into 1-inch pieces
1 tablespoon butter or
   margarine, cut-up
   Paprika

4 servings

For sauce, place butter in 4-cup measure. Microwave at High for 45 seconds to 1 minute, or until butter melts. Stir in flour, salt, lemon pepper and nutmeg. Blend in milk. Microwave at High for 3 to 4½ minutes, or until mixture thickens and bubbles, stirring 3 times. Blend in sour cream. Set aside.

In 1½-quart casserole, combine cod pieces and butter. Cover. Microwave at High for 4 to 7 minutes, or until fish flakes easily with fork, stirring gently after half the time. Drain. Pour sauce over cod. Reduce power to 50% (Medium). Microwave for 2 minutes, or until heated through. Sprinkle with paprika.

Poached Cod with Garlic Mayonnaise

Garlic Mayonnaise:
½ cup mayonnaise
1 teaspoon snipped fresh
   parsley
¼ teaspoon onion powder
⅛ teaspoon minced fresh garlic

2 slices onion, separated into
   rings
¼ cup chopped celery
1 lb. cod fillets, ½ inch thick,
   cut into 4 serving-size
   pieces
¾ cup milk
2 teaspoons snipped fresh
   parsley
¼ teaspoon caraway seed

4 servings

In small mixing bowl, combine all Garlic Mayonnaise ingredients. Mix well. Chill. In 9-inch square baking dish, combine onion and celery. Top with cod fillets. Pour milk over fillets. Sprinkle with parsley and caraway. Cover with plastic wrap. Let stand on counter for 20 to 30 minutes.

Microwave at 70% (Medium High) for 11 to 15 minutes, or until fish flakes easily with fork, rotating dish twice. Let stand, covered, for 2 to 3 minutes. Place cod on serving platter. Serve with Garlic Mayonnaise.

121

◄ Crumb-coated Cod & Vegetables

2 cups fresh broccoli flowerets
1 cup julienne carrots
    (2 × ¼-inch strips)
1 medium potato, thinly sliced
12 oz. cod fillets, about ¾ inch
    thick, cut into 4
    serving-size pieces
1 cup Cheddar cheese
    croutons, crushed
3 tablespoons butter or
    margarine
1 tablespoon snipped fresh
    parsley
⅛ teaspoon garlic powder
⅛ teaspoon pepper

4 servings

In 9-inch square baking dish, combine broccoli, carrots and potato. Cover with plastic wrap. Microwave at High for 5½ to 6½ minutes, or until vegetables are tender-crisp, stirring once. Arrange cod pieces over vegetables. Press crouton crumbs onto cod. Set aside.

In 1-cup measure, combine remaining ingredients. Microwave at High for 45 seconds to 1½ minutes, or until butter melts and mixture begins to boil, stirring after half the time. Drizzle butter mixture over cod and vegetables. Cover with wax paper. Microwave at 70% (Medium High) for 7½ to 11 minutes, or until fish flakes easily with fork, rotating dish after half the time.

Italian Cod ▲

12 oz. cod fillets, about ¾ inch
    thick, cut into 4
    serving-size pieces
1 cup spaghetti sauce
¼ teaspoon dried basil leaves
¼ teaspoon dried oregano
    leaves
⅛ teaspoon garlic powder
⅛ teaspoon pepper
1 cup shredded mozzarella
    cheese
1 tablespoon grated
    Parmesan cheese

4 servings

Arrange cod pieces in 9-inch square baking dish with thickest portions toward outside of dish. Set aside. In small mixing bowl, combine spaghetti sauce, basil, oregano, garlic powder and pepper. Cover. Microwave at High for 1½ to 2 minutes, or until mixture boils, stirring once. Spoon sauce over cod. Sprinkle with mozzarella and Parmesan cheeses. Cover with wax paper. Microwave at 70% (Medium High) for 6 to 9 minutes, or until fish flakes easily with fork, rotating dish after every 2 minutes.

Haddock with Ginger-Lime Butter

12 oz. haddock fillets, about
    ¾ inch thick, cut into 4
    serving-size pieces
¼ cup butter or margarine
½ teaspoon grated lime peel
¼ teaspoon salt
¼ teaspoon finely chopped
    fresh gingerroot
⅛ teaspoon paprika
3 thin lime slices, each cut
    into 4 pieces

4 servings

Arrange haddock pieces in 9-inch square baking dish with thickest portions toward outside of dish. Set aside. In 4-cup measure, combine butter, lime peel, salt, gingerroot and paprika. Microwave at High for 1¾ to 2 minutes, or until butter melts and mixture begins to boil, stirring after half the time. Pour butter mixture over haddock. Top with lime pieces. Cover with wax paper. Microwave at High for 3 to 4½ minutes, or until fish flakes easily with fork, rotating dish after half the time.

Skewered Fish with ▼ Creamy Orange Sauce

1 recipe Creamy Orange Sauce, page 147
12 oz. orange roughy fillets, ½ inch thick
4 wooden skewers, 6-inch

4 servings

Prepare Creamy Orange Sauce as directed. Set aside. Cut orange roughy lengthwise into 1-inch strips. Thread orange roughy strips accordian-style on skewers at 3-inch intervals. Arrange in 9-inch square baking dish. Cover with wax paper. Microwave at High for 3½ to 5 minutes, or until fish flakes easily with fork. Place on serving platter. Remove skewers by twisting and pulling carefully. Spoon Creamy Orange Sauce over fish.

Orange Roughy with Cranberry Sauce

Cranberry Sauce:

1 tablespoon butter or margarine
2 tablespoons finely chopped onion
½ teaspoon grated orange peel
⅛ teaspoon ground allspice
⅛ teaspoon salt
½ cup whole berry cranberry sauce
2 tablespoons fresh orange juice
½ teaspoon honey
Dash pepper

⅓ cup ready-to-serve chicken broth
2 tablespoons white wine vinegar
1 tablespoon vegetable oil
½ teaspoon grated orange peel
Dash pepper
1 lb. orange roughy fillets, ½ inch thick, cut into serving-size pieces

4 to 6 servings

For sauce, in 2-cup measure, combine butter, onion, orange peel and allspice. Microwave at High for 1½ to 2 minutes, or until onion is tender. Stir in remaining sauce ingredients. Reduce power to 50% (Medium). Microwave for 3 to 5 minutes, or until hot and bubbly, stirring once. Cover. Set aside.

In 10-inch square casserole, combine broth, vinegar, oil, orange peel and pepper. Mix well. Arrange orange roughy pieces in casserole with thickest portions toward outside of casserole. Cover. Microwave at High for 5 to 8 minutes, or until fish flakes easily with fork, rearranging fish once. Let stand, covered, for 3 minutes. Spoon Cranberry Sauce over fish.

Orange Roughy
with Vegetables

- 1 medium cucumber, peeled, seeded and cut into 2 × ¼-inch strips
- 1 medium tomato, seeded and chopped
- 1 cup sliced fresh mushrooms
- 1 teaspoon dried tarragon leaves
- 12 oz. orange roughy fillets, ½ inch thick, cut into 4 serving-size pieces
- 2 tablespoons butter or margarine
- 2 tablespoons all-purpose flour
- ¼ teaspoon salt
- ⅛ teaspoon pepper
- ½ cup half-and-half
- ¼ cup white wine
- 1 teaspoon snipped fresh parsley

4 servings

In 9-inch square baking dish, combine cucumber, tomato, mushrooms and tarragon. Cover. Microwave at High for 4 minutes, stirring once. Top with orange roughy pieces. Re-cover. Reduce power to 70% (Medium High). Microwave for 5 to 8 minutes, or until fish flakes easily with fork, turning pieces over after half the time. Drain. Reserve ¼ cup cooking liquid. Set aside. Arrange vegetables and orange roughy on serving platter. Cover. Set aside.

Place butter in 4-cup measure. Microwave at High for 45 seconds to 1 minute, or until butter melts. Stir in flour, salt and pepper. Blend in reserved cooking liquid, half-and-half and wine. Reduce power to 70% (Medium High). Microwave for 2 to 3 minutes, or until mixture thickens and bubbles, stirring after every minute. Pour sauce over orange roughy. Sprinkle with parsley.

Tropical Fillets ▲

¼ cup butter or margarine	⅛ teaspoon ground cinnamon
¼ cup pineapple juice	Dash cayenne
2 teaspoons packed brown sugar	12 oz. red snapper fillets, about ½ inch thick, cut into 4 serving-size pieces
1 teaspoon grated orange peel	¼ cup flaked coconut

4 servings

In small mixing bowl, combine butter, pineapple juice, brown sugar, orange peel, cinnamon and cayenne. Microwave at High for 1½ to 2½ minutes, or until butter melts and mixture boils, stirring after every 30 seconds. Cool slightly. Place red snapper in 9-inch square baking dish. Pour butter mixture over red snapper. Cover. Chill for 2 to 3 hours.

Place coconut in 9-inch round baking dish. Microwave at High for 3 to 4 minutes, or until lightly toasted, stirring often. Set aside. Arrange red snapper pieces on roasting rack with thickest portions toward outside of rack. Microwave at 70% (Medium High) for 7 to 10 minutes, or until fish flakes easily with fork, rotating rack twice. Sprinkle with coconut.

Scandinavian Casserole

3 tablespoons butter or margarine
½ cup chopped red onion
2 tablespoons snipped fresh parsley
1 teaspoon all-purpose flour
½ cup half-and-half
3 cups cubed potatoes, ¾-inch cubes
2 cups flaked smoked fish
⅛ teaspoon pepper
Dash ground nutmeg

6 servings

In 1½-quart casserole, combine butter, onion and parsley. Cover. Microwave at High for 3 to 4 minutes, or until onion is tender, stirring once. Stir in flour. Blend in half-and-half. Stir in potatoes, fish, pepper and nutmeg. Re-cover. Microwave at High for 13 to 18 minutes, or until potatoes are tender, stirring twice. Let stand, covered, for 5 minutes. Serve with butter and snipped fresh parsley.

Sole with ▶ Swiss Cheese Sauce

1 small zucchini, cut in half
lengthwise, sliced ¼ inch
thick
½ cup sliced celery, ¼ inch
thick

Swiss Cheese Sauce:

2 tablespoons butter or
margarine
1 tablespoon sliced green
onion
2 teaspoons snipped fresh
parsley
¼ teaspoon salt
⅛ teaspoon dried marjoram
leaves
Dash pepper
2 tablespoons all-purpose flour
1 cup milk
1 cup shredded Swiss cheese

1 lb. sole fillets, about ¾ inch
thick, cut into serving-size
pieces

4 to 6 servings

In 9-inch square baking dish,
combine zucchini and celery.
Cover with plastic wrap. Microwave at High for 3 to 4 minutes,
or until tender-crisp, stirring
once. Set aside.

For sauce, in 4 cup measure,
combine butter, onion, parsley,
salt, marjoram and pepper.
Microwave at High for 1 to 1¼
minutes, or until butter melts. Stir
in flour. Blend in milk. Microwave
at High for 3 to 4½ minutes, or
until mixture thickens and
bubbles, stirring 3 times. Stir
in cheese until melted.

Arrange sole pieces in 9-inch
square baking dish with thickest
portions toward outside of dish.
Spoon zucchini and celery over
sole. Pour cheese sauce over
sole and vegetables. Microwave, uncovered, at High for
7 to 11 minutes, or until fish
flakes easily with fork,
rearranging pieces after
half the time.

Grouper in Herb Butter

1 lb. grouper fillets, about
1 inch thick, cut into 4
serving-size pieces
¼ cup butter or margarine
1 teaspoon lemon juice
½ teaspoon dried parsley
flakes

⅛ teaspoon Italian seasoning
Dash garlic powder
Dash fennel seed, crushed
1 to 2 tablespoons grated
Parmesan cheese

4 servings

Arrange grouper pieces in 9-inch square baking dish with thickest
portions toward outside of dish. Set aside. In 1-cup measure, combine butter, lemon juice, parsley, Italian seasoning, garlic powder
and fennel. Microwave at High for 1 to 1½ minutes, or until butter
melts. Pour over grouper pieces. Cover with wax paper. Microwave
at High for 6 to 10 minutes, or until fish flakes easily with fork,
rotating dish twice. Sprinkle with Parmesan cheese. Let stand,
covered, for 2 to 3 minutes.

◄ Bouillabaisse American-style

2 tablespoons olive oil
1 medium onion, chopped
1 medium green pepper, chopped
2 cloves garlic, minced
3 medium tomatoes, seeded and chopped
8 oz. fresh mushrooms, cut in half
1 can (14½ oz.) ready-to-serve chicken broth
½ cup white wine or water
½ teaspoon salt
½ teaspoon dried thyme leaves

¼ teaspoon fennel seed, crushed
⅛ to ¼ teaspoon powdered saffron
⅛ teaspoon cayenne
2 bay leaves
1 lobster tail, about ½ lb.
¾ lb. cooked crab legs
1 dozen small hard-shell clams, scrubbed
12 oz. cod or haddock fillets, cut into 1-inch cubes
¾ lb. medium shrimp, shelled and deveined
½ lb. bay scallops

10 to 12 servings

In 5-quart casserole, combine olive oil, onion, green pepper and garlic. Stir. Cover. Microwave at High for 3 to 4 minutes, or until onion is tender-crisp, stirring once. Add tomatoes, mushrooms, broth, wine, salt, thyme, fennel, saffron, cayenne and bay leaves. Stir. Re-cover. Microwave at High for 5 minutes. Reduce power to 70% (Medium High). Microwave for 25 to 30 minutes, or until flavors are blended, stirring occasionally.

Using kitchen shears or sharp knife, cut lobster shell in half lengthwise. Cut through center of lobster flesh. Cut crab legs into 3 or 4-inch pieces. Add lobster, crab and remaining ingredients to casserole. Stir. Re-cover. Microwave at 70% (Medium High) for 15 to 20 minutes, or until clams begin to open and shrimp and scallops are opaque, stirring twice. Let stand, covered, for 5 minutes. Remove bay leaves before serving.

Lobster Tails with Orange Butter

1 recipe Orange Butter, page 151
2 lobster tails (about ½ lb. each)

2 tablespoons water
2 tablespoons white wine

2 servings

Prepare Orange Butter as directed. Set aside. Using kitchen shears or sharp knife, remove thin covering from underside of each lobster tail. Cut lengthwise slit through center of lobster flesh. Separate flesh along slit. Place lobster tails shell-side down in 9-inch square baking dish. Pour 1 tablespoon Orange Butter along slit in each lobster tail. Reserve remaining butter. In 1-cup measure, combine water and wine. Pour around lobster tails. Cover with plastic wrap. Microwave at 50% (Medium) for 6 to 10 minutes, or until lobster is opaque, rotating dish 2 or 3 times. Let stand, covered, for 3 to 4 minutes. Serve with warm Orange Butter.

Shrimp & Couscous

Couscous:
1 tablespoon olive oil
¼ cup sliced green onions
2 tablespoons snipped fresh parsley
⅛ teaspoon garlic powder
⅛ teaspoon pepper
1 cup ready-to-serve chicken broth
1 cup uncooked couscous

Sauce:
1 can (28 oz.) whole tomatoes, drained and cut-up
½ teaspoon dried basil leaves
¼ teaspoon salt
¼ teaspoon dried oregano leaves
⅛ teaspoon garlic powder
⅛ teaspoon cayenne
2 tablespoons olive oil
2 tablespoons butter or margarine
1 tablespoon all-purpose flour
¾ lb. large shrimp, shelled and deveined

4 servings

For couscous, in 1-quart casserole, combine olive oil, onions, parsley, garlic powder, pepper and broth. Cover. Microwave at High for 4 to 6 minutes, or until mixture boils. Stir in couscous. Re-cover. Set aside. For sauce, in 2-quart casserole, combine all ingredients, except flour and shrimp. Cover. Microwave at High for 5 to 6 minutes, or until mixture is very hot, stirring after half the time. Blend in flour. Stir in shrimp. Re-cover. Reduce power to 70% (Medium High). Microwave for 4 to 9 minutes, or until shrimp are opaque, stirring after every 3 minutes. Serve sauce over couscous.

Shrimp Moutarde

Marinade:
¼ cup olive oil
2 tablespoons red wine
    vinegar
2 teaspoons Dijon mustard
1 teaspoon dried parsley
    flakes

1 teaspoon freeze-dried chives
½ teaspoon sugar
    Dash pepper
1 lb. extra-large shrimp,
    shelled and deveined

3 to 4 servings

In small mixing bowl, blend all marinade ingredients. In large plastic food storage bag, combine marinade and shrimp. Secure bag. Marinate in refrigerator for 3 hours. Pour shrimp and marinade into 2-quart casserole. Cover. Microwave at 70% (Medium High) for 6 to 9 minutes, or until shrimp are opaque, stirring after every 2 minutes. Let stand, covered, for 2 to 3 minutes.

Saucy Shrimp & Vegetables

¼ cup butter or margarine
2 cups thinly sliced bok choy
1 medium yellow summer
    squash, cut into
    2 × ¼-inch strips
1 cup sliced fresh mushrooms
1 can (16 oz.) whole tomatoes,
    drained and cut-up
1 tablespoon white wine

¾ teaspoon bouquet garni
    seasoning
½ teaspoon salt
¼ teaspoon garlic powder
¼ teaspoon pepper
1 tablespoon all-purpose flour
¾ lb. medium shrimp, shelled,
    deveined and butterflied
¼ cup whipping cream

4 servings

In 2-quart casserole, combine butter, bok choy, squash, mushrooms and tomatoes. Cover. Microwave at High for 5½ to 6½ minutes, or until vegetables are tender-crisp, stirring after every 2 minutes. Remove vegetables with slotted spoon. Set aside. Reserve cooking liquid in casserole. Add wine, bouquet garni, salt, garlic powder and pepper. Stir in flour. Add shrimp. Re-cover. Reduce power to 50% (Medium). Microwave for 6 to 8 minutes, or until shrimp are opaque, stirring after every 2 minutes. Stir in vegetable mixture. Blend in cream. Microwave, uncovered, at 50% (Medium) for 4 to 5 minutes, or until heated through, stirring after half the time. Serve over hot cooked noodles or rice.

Cajun Shrimp ▶

Crumb Topping:
1 tablespoon butter or
    margarine
¼ cup unseasoned dry bread
    crumbs
⅛ teaspoon pepper
    Dash cayenne

½ cup chopped green pepper
¼ cup sliced green onions
1 clove garlic, minced
¼ teaspoon dry mustard
¼ teaspoon chili powder
⅛ teaspoon dried thyme leaves
1 can (8 oz.) tomato sauce
½ lb. medium shrimp, shelled
    and deveined
¼ lb. bay scallops
¼ teaspoon salt
¼ teaspoon sugar

4 servings

For topping, place butter in custard cup. Microwave at High for 30 seconds to 1 minute, or until butter melts. Stir in remaining topping ingredients. Set aside.

In 1-quart casserole, combine green pepper, onions, garlic, dry mustard, chili powder and thyme. Cover. Microwave at High for 2 to 4 minutes, or until onion is tender, stirring once. Stir in tomato sauce, shrimp, scallops, salt and sugar. Spoon into 4 individual soufflé dishes or casseroles. Microwave at 70% (Medium High) for 8 to 13 minutes, or until shrimp and scallops are opaque, rearranging dishes twice. Add crumb topping during last minute of cooking time.

Shrimp Brunch Ring

8 slices white bread, lightly toasted
1 can (4¼ oz.) large shrimp, drained
1 cup fresh broccoli flowerets
½ cup shredded Monterey Jack cheese
½ cup shredded mild Cheddar cheese
2 tablespoons finely chopped onion
4 eggs, beaten
1 cup milk
½ teaspoon salt
½ teaspoon freeze-dried chives
¼ teaspoon dry mustard
⅛ teaspoon pepper

6 to 8 servings

How to Microwave Shrimp Brunch Ring

Trim each slice of toast to form a square. Cut each slice in half diagonally to form 2 triangles. Cut bread trimmings into ½-inch cubes to equal 1 cup. Set aside.

Fit toast triangles over bottom of 9-inch ring dish, overlapping triangles. Set aside.

Combine reserved bread cubes, shrimp, broccoli, Monterey Jack and Cheddar cheeses and onion in medium mixing bowl. Spoon into toast-lined ring dish, packing slightly.

Blend eggs, milk, salt, chives, dry mustard and pepper in 4-cup measure. Pour evenly over filling in ring dish. Cover with plastic wrap. Chill for at least 6 hours or overnight.

Microwave, uncovered, at High for 3 minutes. Rotate dish half turn. Reduce power to 70% (Medium High).

Microwave for 11 to 17 minutes, or until set and knife inserted in center comes out clean, rotating dish twice. Let stand, covered, for 5 minutes.

◄ Shrimp Pasta Sauce

3 tablespoons olive oil
⅔ cup chopped fresh
  mushrooms
½ cup cubed zucchini, ½-inch
  cubes
¼ cup finely chopped onion
2 tablespoons snipped fresh
  parsley
1 clove garlic, minced
½ teaspoon dried basil leaves
¼ teaspoon dried thyme leaves
1 can (16 oz.) whole tomatoes
1 can (6 oz.) tomato paste
¼ teaspoon salt
¼ teaspoon sugar
¼ teaspoon pepper
½ lb. extra-small shrimp,
  shelled and deveined

4 to 6 servings

In 2-quart casserole, combine
olive oil, mushrooms, zucchini,
onion, parsley, garlic, basil and
thyme. Cover. Microwave at
High for 3 to 6 minutes, or until
vegetables are tender, stirring
once. Add remaining ingredients, except shrimp, stirring to
break apart tomatoes. Cover
with wax paper. Reduce power
to 70% (Medium High). Microwave for 10 to 15 minutes, or
until flavors are blended, stirring
once. Stir in shrimp. Re-cover.
Microwave at 70% (Medium
High) for 3 to 4 minutes, or until
shrimp are opaque, stirring
once. Let stand, covered, for
3 minutes. Serve over hot
cooked pasta.

Oysters Deluxe

2 slices bacon
2 tablespoons butter or
  margarine
½ cup chopped red pepper
¼ cup finely chopped onion
¼ teaspoon dried marjoram
  leaves
2 tablespoons all-purpose
  flour
⅔ cup half-and-half
1½ teaspoons lemon juice
¾ teaspoon salt
¼ teaspoon dry mustard
4 to 5 drops hot pepper
  sauce
1 pint fresh oysters, drained

4 servings

Place bacon on paper towel-
lined plate. Cover with another
paper towel. Microwave at High
for 2 to 2½ minutes, or until
crisp and brown. Cool slightly.
Crumble. Set aside.

In 1-quart casserole, combine
butter, red pepper, onion and
marjoram. Cover. Microwave at
High for 3 to 5 minutes, or until
vegetables are tender, stirring
once. Stir in flour. Blend in
half-and-half. Stir in lemon juice,
salt, dry mustard and hot
pepper sauce. Reduce power
to 70% (Medium High). Microwave for 3 to 5 minutes, or until
mixture thickens and bubbles,
stirring twice. Mixture will be
very thick. Stir in oysters.
Reduce power to 50% (Medium).
Microwave for 6 to 10 minutes,
or until oysters are firm and
edges begin to curl, stirring
twice. Serve over toast points.
Sprinkle with bacon.

Oyster Casserole

2 tablespoons butter or
  margarine
½ cup chopped onion
½ cup chopped celery
½ cup chopped green pepper
¼ cup snipped fresh parsley
½ teaspoon salt
⅛ teaspoon pepper
⅛ teaspoon cayenne
1 cup oyster crackers, crushed
1 can (8 oz.) whole tomatoes,
  drained and cut-up
¼ cup ketchup
1 tablespoon all-purpose flour
2 eggs, slightly beaten
1 pint fresh oysters, drained
  and chopped (reserve
  ¼ cup oyster liquor)

Topping:

2 tablespoons butter or
  margarine
⅛ teaspoon cayenne
1 cup oyster crackers

4 to 6 servings

In 2-quart casserole, combine
butter, onion, celery, green
pepper, parsley, salt, pepper
and cayenne. Cover. Microwave
at High for 5 to 6 minutes, or
until vegetables are tender,
stirring after every 2 minutes.
Add cracker crumbs, tomatoes,
ketchup, flour and eggs. Mix
well. Stir in oysters and
reserved liquor. Set aside.

For topping, place butter in
small mixing bowl. Microwave at
High for 45 seconds to 1 minute,
or until butter melts. Stir in
cayenne and crackers. Toss to
coat. Arrange topping around
outside edge of casserole.
Microwave at 50% (Medium) for
18 to 28 minutes, or until heated
through, rotating casserole after
every 5 minutes. Let stand,
covered, for 5 minutes.

◀ Scallops with Wine & Cheese Sauce

1 lb. bay scallops
⅓ cup white wine
3 tablespoons butter or margarine
½ teaspoon dry mustard
¼ teaspoon garlic powder, divided
2 cups shredded Colby cheese
1 tablespoon all-purpose flour
¼ cup seeded chopped tomato
1 tablespoon snipped fresh parsley
1 tablespoon sliced green onion
1 teaspoon olive oil
4 English muffins, split and toasted

4 servings

Place scallops in 9-inch square baking dish. Cover with plastic wrap. Microwave at 50% (Medium) for 6 to 9 minutes, or until scallops are opaque, stirring 2 or 3 times. Set aside. In 2-quart casserole, combine wine, butter, dry mustard and ⅛ teaspoon garlic powder. Microwave at High for 2½ to 3½ minutes, or until mixture boils. In large plastic food storage bag, combine cheese and flour. Shake to coat. Stir into wine and butter mixture. Reduce power to 50% (Medium). Microwave for 1½ to 2 minutes, or until mixture can be stirred smooth, stirring after every minute. Drain scallops. Stir scallops into cheese sauce. Microwave at 50% (Medium) for 1 to 2 minutes, or until heated through. In small mixing bowl, combine tomato, parsley, onion, olive oil and remaining ⅛ teaspoon garlic powder. Mix well. Spoon scallops and cheese sauce over English muffins. Top with tomato mixture.

Creamy Scallops in Patty Shells ▲

8 frozen patty shells
2 tablespoons butter or margarine
2 tablespoons finely chopped celery
1 tablespoon finely chopped green onion
2 tablespoons all-purpose flour

1¼ cups milk
1 cup sliced fresh mushrooms
½ teaspoon salt
½ teaspoon Worcestershire sauce
¼ teaspoon dried tarragon leaves
Dash cayenne
½ lb. bay scallops

4 servings

Bake patty shells according to package directions. Set aside. In 1½-quart casserole, combine butter, celery and onion. Cover. Microwave at High for 3 to 4 minutes, or until tender, stirring once. Stir in flour. Blend in milk. Stir in mushrooms, salt, Worcestershire sauce, tarragon and cayenne. Microwave, uncovered, at High for 5 to 7 minutes, or until mixture thickens and bubbles, stirring after every 2 minutes. Stir in scallops. Reduce power to 70% (Medium High). Microwave for 4 to 6 minutes, or until scallops are firm and opaque, stirring once. Spoon into prepared patty shells.

Creole Clam Omelet

2 tablespoons butter or
    margarine, divided
⅓ cup chopped green pepper
⅓ cup chopped celery
2 tablespoons chopped onion
½ teaspoon dried oregano
    leaves
1 tablespoon chopped
    pimiento, drained
⅛ teaspoon pepper
1 can (6½ oz.) minced clams,
    drained
2 slices bacon
4 eggs, separated
2 tablespoons milk
¼ teaspoon baking powder
⅛ teaspoon paprika
½ cup shredded Cheddar
    cheese

2 to 4 servings

In small mixing bowl, combine 1 tablespoon butter, green pepper, celery, onion and oregano. Cover. Microwave at High for 3 to 4 minutes, or until vegetables are tender, stirring after half the time. Stir in pimiento, pepper and clams. Set aside. Place bacon on paper towel-lined plate. Cover with another paper towel. Microwave at High for 2 to 3 minutes, or until crisp. Cool slightly. Crumble. Add to vegetable mixture. Set aside.

In large mixing bowl, beat egg whites at high speed of electric mixer until stiff but not dry. Set aside. In small mixing bowl, combine egg yolks, milk and baking powder. Beat until thick and lemon-colored. Gently fold egg yolk mixture into egg whites, using a rubber spatula.

In 9-inch pie plate, combine remaining 1 tablespoon butter and paprika. Microwave at High for 45 seconds to 1 minute, or until butter melts. Tilt plate to coat bottom and sides. Pour egg mixture into pie plate. Place on saucer in microwave oven. Reduce power to 50% (Medium). Microwave for 5½ to 7½ minutes, or until set, lifting edges with spatula after every 2 minutes so uncooked portion spreads evenly. Sprinkle clam filling over half of omelet. Loosen omelet with spatula and fold in half. Sprinkle with cheese. Microwave at 50% (Medium) for 1½ to 2 minutes, or until cheese melts.

Clam Pilaf ▲

1 pkg. (9 oz.) frozen cut green beans
2 tablespoons butter or margarine
1 tablespoon olive oil
2 medium potatoes, cut into ½-inch cubes
¼ cup chopped onion
1 tablespoon snipped fresh parsley
¾ teaspoon salt
½ teaspoon dried thyme leaves
⅛ teaspoon pepper
3 cups hot cooked wild rice
2 cans (6½ oz. each) minced clams, drained

4 to 6 servings

Unwrap beans and place on plate. Microwave at High for 4 to 5 minutes, or until defrosted. Drain. Set aside. In 2-quart casserole, combine butter, olive oil, potatoes, onion, parsley, salt, thyme and pepper. Cover. Microwave at High for 6 to 8 minutes, or until potatoes are tender, stirring after every 2 minutes. Stir in beans, wild rice and clams. Re-cover. Reduce power to 70% (Medium High). Microwave for 2½ to 3½ minutes, or until heated through, stirring after half the time.

Crab Cakes with Cheddar Cheese Sauce

Crab Cakes:
1 tablespoon butter or margarine
¼ cup chopped onion
¼ cup finely shredded carrot
2 tablespoons chopped green pepper
2 teaspoons snipped fresh parsley
1 can (6 oz.) crab meat, rinsed, drained and cartilage removed
1½ cups oyster crackers, crushed
1 egg, beaten
½ cup mayonnaise
1 teaspoon Dijon mustard
¼ teaspoon salt
⅛ teaspoon garlic powder
½ cup cornflake crumbs

Cheddar Cheese Sauce:
2 tablespoons butter or margarine
2 tablespoons all-purpose flour
¼ teaspoon salt
⅛ teaspoon cayenne
½ teaspoon Dijon mustard
1 cup milk
1 cup shredded Cheddar cheese

4 servings

For crab cakes, in medium mixing bowl, combine butter, onion, carrot, green pepper and parsley. Cover. Microwave at High for 2 to 3 minutes, or until vegetables are tender, stirring once. Add remaining crab cake ingredients, except cornflake crumbs. Mix well. Shape into 4 patties, about 1 inch thick. Dip both sides of each patty in cornflake crumbs, pressing lightly to coat. Arrange on roasting rack. Set aside.

For sauce, place butter in 4-cup measure. Microwave at High for 45 seconds to 1 minute, or until butter melts. Stir in flour, salt, cayenne and mustard. Blend in milk. Microwave at High for 3 to 4 minutes, or until mixture thickens and bubbles, stirring after every minute. Stir in cheese until melted. Cover. Set aside.

For crab cakes, microwave at 70% (Medium High) for 5 to 9 minutes, or until firm, rotating rack after every 3 minutes. Serve with Cheddar Cheese Sauce.

Seafood Asparagus Bake

½ cup sliced almonds
1 tablespoon butter or margarine
1 pkg. (10 oz.) frozen asparagus cuts
⅓ cup thinly sliced celery
¼ cup chopped onion
1½ cups instant rice
1½ cups milk
1 can (10¾ oz.) condensed cream of shrimp soup
1 can (6 oz.) crab meat, rinsed, drained and cartilage removed
1 can (4¼ oz.) small shrimp, drained
1 tablespoon fresh lemon juice
½ teaspoon grated lemon peel
¼ teaspoon dried dill weed
⅛ teaspoon pepper

6 to 8 servings

In 9-inch round baking dish, combine almonds and butter. Microwave at High for 4 to 5 minutes, or just until almonds begin to brown, stirring once. Set aside. Unwrap asparagus and place on plate. Microwave at High for 3 to 5 minutes, or until defrosted. Drain. Set aside.

In 2-quart casserole, combine celery and onion. Cover. Microwave at High for 2½ to 3½ minutes, or until tender-crisp, stirring once. Stir in asparagus and remaining ingredients, except toasted almonds. Mix well. Re-cover. Microwave at High for 10 to 15 minutes, or until mixture boils, stirring after every 5 minutes. Stir in almonds. Let stand, covered, for 5 minutes.

Salmon & ▶ Mostaccioli Bake

2 cups uncooked mostaccioli

Sauce:

2 tablespoons butter or margarine
2 tablespoons all-purpose flour
1½ cups milk
1 teaspoon instant minced onion
½ teaspoon salt
¼ teaspoon dried dill weed
¼ teaspoon lemon pepper seasoning

1 can (7½ oz.) salmon, drained and flaked
½ cup shredded Swiss cheese
½ cup frozen peas
2 tablespoons sliced almonds

4 servings

Cook and rinse mostaccioli according to package directions. Set aside. Place butter in 1½-quart casserole. Microwave at High for 45 seconds to 1 minute, or until butter melts. Stir in flour. Blend in milk. Stir in onion, salt, dill and lemon pepper. Microwave at High for 4 to 6 minutes, or until mixture thickens and bubbles, stirring twice. Remove bones and skin from salmon. Stir salmon, mostaccioli, cheese and peas into sauce. Cover. Reduce power to 70% (Medium High). Microwave for 5 to 8 minutes, or until heated through. Sprinkle with sliced almonds.

Tuna & Mostaccioli Bake:
Follow recipe above, substituting 1 can (6½ oz.) tuna, drained, for salmon.

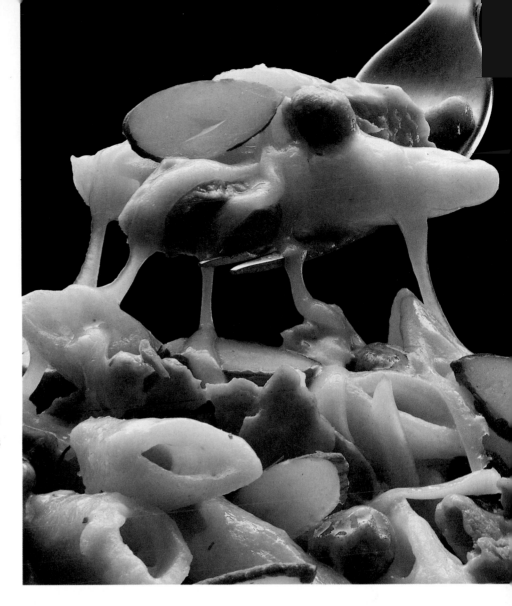

Linguine & Tuna

7 oz. uncooked linguine
2 tablespoons butter or margarine
2 cups sliced fresh mushrooms
¼ cup sliced green onions
½ teaspoon dried basil leaves
2 tablespoons snipped fresh parsley

½ teaspoon salt
¼ teaspoon pepper
2 eggs, beaten
⅔ cup evaporated milk
1 can (6½ oz.) tuna, drained
Snipped fresh parsley (optional)

4 servings

Cook and rinse linguine according to package directions. Set aside. In 2-quart casserole, combine butter, mushrooms, onions and basil. Cover. Microwave at High for 3½ to 5½ minutes, or just until mushrooms are tender, stirring once. Add linguine, parsley, salt and pepper. Toss to coat. In small mixing bowl, blend eggs and evaporated milk. Pour over linguine. Toss to coat. Microwave, uncovered, at High for 3½ to 9 minutes, or until mixture is thickened and creamy, stirring well after first 2 minutes, then after every minute. Add flaked tuna. Gently toss to mix. Let stand, covered, for 1 minute. Garnish with snipped parsley.

Cheesy Tuna Taters

4 large baking potatoes (8 to 9 oz. each)
¼ cup butter or margarine
1 tablespoon sliced green onion
1 tablespoon finely chopped celery
2 teaspoons snipped fresh parsley
¼ cup dairy sour cream
2 tablespoons half-and-half or milk
1 teaspoon freeze-dried chives
½ teaspoon salt
⅛ teaspoon pepper
1 can (6½ oz.) tuna, drained
½ cup finely shredded Cheddar cheese, divided

4 servings

Pierce potatoes with fork. Arrange in circular pattern on paper towel in microwave oven. Microwave at High for 12 to 16 minutes, or until tender, turning potatoes over and rearranging after half the time. Let stand, wrapped in foil, for 10 minutes.

In medium mixing bowl, combine butter, onion, celery and parsley. Microwave at High for 2 to 3 minutes, or until vegetables are tender, stirring once. Slice tops off potatoes. Scoop out pulp, leaving ¼-inch shell. Add pulp to vegetable mixture. Arrange shells on paper towel-lined plate. Set aside. Add sour cream, half-and-half, chives, salt and pepper to vegetable mixture. Beat until smooth and fluffy. Stir in tuna and ¼ cup Cheddar cheese. Spoon mixture into potato shells, mounding slightly. Sprinkle with remaining ¼ cup cheese. Microwave at High for 3 to 5 minutes, or until heated through and cheese melts, rotating plate once.

Seafood Roll-ups ▶

6 uncooked lasagna noodles

Filling:
¾ cup ricotta cheese
1 egg, beaten
2 tablespoons grated Parmesan cheese
½ teaspoon dried parsley flakes
¼ teaspoon salt
¼ teaspoon Italian seasoning
½ lb. seafood sticks, cut-up

Sauce:
1 can (16 oz.) whole tomatoes, cut-up
1 can (6 oz.) tomato paste
1 teaspoon instant minced onion
½ teaspoon Italian seasoning
½ teaspoon dried parsley flakes
½ teaspoon sugar
¼ teaspoon salt
⅛ teaspoon garlic powder

1 cup shredded mozzarella cheese

6 servings

Cook and rinse lasagna noodles according to package directions. Place noodles flat on plastic wrap. Set aside. In small mixing bowl, combine all filling ingredients, except seafood sticks. Spread about 3 tablespoons of filling on each lasagna noodle. Sprinkle seafood over filling. Set aside. In 1½-quart casserole, combine all sauce ingredients. Microwave at High for 9 to 11 minutes, or until sauce thickens. Spread 2 tablespoons sauce over each filled noodle. Roll up each noodle, enclosing filling. Place seam-side down in 9-inch square baking dish. Spread remaining sauce over roll-ups. Cover with wax paper. Microwave at High for 10 to 15 minutes, or until heated through, rotating dish twice. Sprinkle with mozzarella cheese. Reduce power to 50% (Medium). Microwave for 3 to 4 minutes, or until cheese melts.

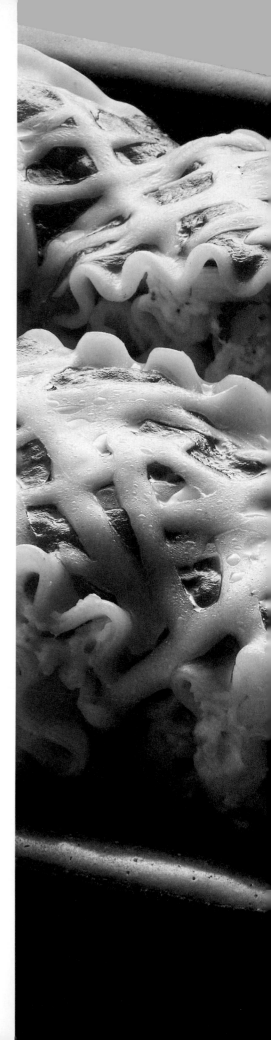

Sauces

Fresh Vegetable Sauce ▲

2 medium tomatoes, seeded
   and cut into wedges
½ cup shredded carrots
¼ cup chopped onion
2 tablespoons snipped fresh
   parsley
1 clove garlic, cut in half
3 tablespoons tomato paste
½ teaspoon salt
½ teaspoon sugar
¼ teaspoon dried crushed
   sage leaves
⅛ teaspoon pepper
   Dash ground nutmeg

About 1½ cups

In food processor or blender
container, combine tomatoes,
carrots, onion, parsley and
garlic. Process until smooth.
Pour into 1-quart casserole. Stir
in remaining ingredients. Microwave at High for 15 to 20 minutes, or until slightly thickened,
stirring 2 or 3 times. Serve hot
over fish fillets, chicken breasts
or turkey cutlets.

Cream Sauce

1½ cups half-and-half
⅛ teaspoon ground nutmeg
1 bay leaf
2 tablespoons butter or
   margarine
2 tablespoons all-purpose
   flour
¼ teaspoon salt
⅛ teaspoon pepper

1½ cups

In 2-cup measure, combine
half-and-half, nutmeg and bay
leaf. Microwave at 70% (Medium
High) for 3½ to 4½ minutes, or
until hot but not boiling, stirring
1 or 2 times. Remove bay leaf.
Set aside. Place butter in 4-cup
measure. Microwave at High for
45 seconds to 1 minute, or until
butter melts. Stir in flour, salt
and pepper. Blend in half-and-
half mixture. Reduce power to
70% (Medium High). Microwave
for 1½ to 2½ minutes, or until
mixture thickens and bubbles,
stirring after the first 30 seconds
and then after every minute.
Serve with fish, seafood
or chicken.

Tartar Sauce

2 tablespoons chopped onion
½ teaspoon freeze-dried
   chives
½ teaspoon vegetable oil
¼ teaspoon celery salt
   Dash pepper
½ cup mayonnaise
2 tablespoons dairy sour
   cream
2 tablespoons finely chopped
   dill or sweet pickle
1½ teaspoons lemon juice

¾ cup

In small mixing bowl, combine
onion, chives, oil, celery salt
and pepper. Cover. Microwave
at High for 1 to 1½ minutes, or
until onion is tender-crisp. Cool
slightly. Blend in remaining ingredients. Re-cover. Chill for at
least 30 minutes to blend flavors.
Serve with fish or seafood.

Creamy Orange Sauce ▲

- 2 tablespoons butter or margarine
- 2 tablespoons sliced green onion
- 2 teaspoons snipped fresh parsley
- 1 teaspoon grated orange peel
- 1 tablespoon all-purpose flour
- ¼ teaspoon salt
- ¼ teaspoon dry mustard
- ¾ cup milk
- 1 tablespoon fresh orange juice

About 1 cup

In 2-cup measure, combine butter, onion, parsley and orange peel. Microwave at High for 1 to 1¼ minutes, or until butter melts. Stir in flour, salt and mustard. Blend in milk. Microwave at High for 2½ to 4 minutes, or until mixture thickens and bubbles, stirring after every minute. Stir in orange juice. Serve over fish or chicken.

Clam Sauce

- ¼ cup butter or margarine
- ¼ cup snipped fresh parsley
- ¼ cup finely chopped onion
- 1 clove garlic, minced
- 2 tablespoons olive oil
- ¼ teaspoon salt
- ¼ teaspoon pepper
- 1 tablespoon all-purpose flour
- ¼ cup half-and-half
- 1 can (6½ oz.) minced clams, drained (reserve liquid)

About 1 cup

In small mixing bowl, combine butter, parsley, onion, garlic, olive oil, salt and pepper. Cover with plastic wrap. Microwave at High for 2 to 4 minutes, or until onion is tender. Stir in flour. Blend in half-and-half and reserved clam liquid. Microwave, uncovered, at High for 2 to 4 minutes, or until mixture thickens and bubbles, stirring after every minute. Stir in clams. Serve over hot cooked linguine.

Barbecue Sauce

- 4 slices bacon, cut-up
- 1 medium apple, peeled and chopped
- ½ cup chopped onion
- ½ teaspoon dried basil leaves
- ½ teaspoon dry mustard
- ¼ teaspoon garlic powder
- ¼ teaspoon pepper
- ¼ teaspoon dried crushed red pepper
- 1 can (15 oz.) tomato sauce
- ⅓ cup honey
- ¼ cup steak sauce

About 3 cups

Place bacon in 2-quart casserole. Microwave at High for 4 to 7 minutes, or until crisp, stirring after half the time. Drain. Reserve 1 tablespoon bacon fat. In same casserole, combine bacon, reserved fat, apple, onion, basil, mustard, garlic powder, pepper and red pepper. Cover. Microwave at High for 4 to 5 minutes, or until apple and onion are tender. Stir in remaining ingredients. Microwave, uncovered, at High for 6 to 9 minutes, or until mixture begins to boil, stirring 2 or 3 times. Serve with fish or poultry.

◄ Creamy Lemon-Tarragon Sauce

- 2 tablespoons butter or margarine
- 1 tablespoon finely chopped onion
- ½ teaspoon salt
- ½ teaspoon grated lemon peel
- ¼ teaspoon dried tarragon leaves
- 2 tablespoons all-purpose flour
- 1⅓ cups milk
- 4 to 6 drops hot pepper sauce
- 1 egg yolk, beaten

1⅓ cups

In 4-cup measure, combine butter, onion, salt, lemon peel and tarragon. Cover with plastic wrap. Microwave at High for 2 to 2½ minutes, or until butter melts. Stir in flour. Blend in milk and hot pepper sauce. Microwave, uncovered, at High for 3½ to 5½ minutes, or until mixture begins to boil, stirring after every minute. Blend small amount of hot mixture into egg yolk. Return egg yolk mixture to hot mixture, blending with whisk. Reduce power to 50% (Medium). Microwave for 1 to 1½ minutes, or just until thickened, stirring twice. Serve with fish or chicken.

Spicy Cocktail Sauce

- ½ cup chili sauce
- ¼ cup finely chopped celery
- 2 teaspoons frozen grapefruit juice concentrate
- 1 teaspoon grated onion
- ¾ teaspoon sugar
- ½ teaspoon prepared horseradish
- ¼ teaspoon Worcestershire sauce
  Dash cayenne

¾ cup

In small mixing bowl, combine all ingredients. Mix well. Chill. Serve with fish or seafood.

Golden Raisin Sauce ▶

⅓ cup packed brown sugar
1 tablespoon cornstarch
1 cup apple juice
⅓ cup golden raisins
¼ teaspoon caraway seed
¼ teaspoon grated orange peel

1½ cups

In 4-cup measure, combine
brown sugar and cornstarch.
Mix well. Stir in remaining ingredients. Microwave at High for
2 to 4 minutes, or until mixture
thickens and bubbles, stirring
after every minute. Serve with
poultry or fish.

Dilly Mayonnaise

2 tablespoons sliced green
  onion
1 tablespoon snipped fresh
  parsley
½ teaspoon vegetable oil
¼ teaspoon lemon pepper
  seasoning
¼ teaspoon dried dill weed
½ cup mayonnaise
⅛ teaspoon salt

⅔ cup

In small mixing bowl, combine
onion, parsley, oil, lemon pepper
and dill weed. Cover with plastic
wrap. Microwave at High for 45
seconds to 1 minute, or until
onion is tender-crisp. Cool
slightly. Blend in mayonnaise
and salt. Re-cover. Chill for at
least 30 minutes to blend
flavors. Serve with fish fillets
or seafood.

Dilly-Caper Mayonnaise:
Follow recipe above, except
add 1 tablespoon drained
capers with mayonnaise.
Omit salt.

Chili Mayonnaise ▲

- 2 tablespoons finely chopped celery
- 2 tablespoons chili sauce
- ½ teaspoon chili powder
- ½ teaspoon paprika
  Dash cayenne
- ½ cup mayonnaise

⅔ cup

In small mixing bowl, combine all ingredients, except mayonnaise. Mix well. Cover with plastic wrap. Microwave at High for 1½ to 2 minutes, or until celery is tender-crisp. Cool slightly. Blend in mayonnaise. Re-cover. Chill for at least 30 minutes to blend flavors. Serve with fish or seafood.

Pineapple-Orange Marinade

- 1 can (16 oz.) unsweetened pineapple juice
- 2 tablespoons vegetable oil
- 1 tablespoon Worcestershire sauce
- 1 tablespoon dark corn syrup
- 1 teaspoon grated orange peel
- ½ teaspoon salt
- ⅛ teaspoon ground allspice
- ⅛ teaspoon ground cinnamon
  Dash cayenne

1 cup

In 2-cup measure, combine all ingredients. Mix well. Microwave at High for 1½ to 2½ minutes, or until mixture boils. Cool slightly. Pour over chicken pieces. Cover. Chill for 6 to 8 hours to marinate. Remove chicken from marinade. Microwave as directed on page 19.

Sweet & Spicy Marinade

- ½ cup Russian dressing
- ½ cup orange marmalade
- 2 tablespoons finely chopped onion
- ½ teaspoon Worcestershire sauce

About 1 cup

In small mixing bowl, combine all ingredients. Mix well. Microwave at High for 2 to 3 minutes, or until mixture boils, stirring after half the time. Cool slightly. Pour over chicken pieces or cod fillets. Cover. Chill for 2 to 3 hours to marinate. Remove chicken from marinade. Microwave as directed on page 19 or page 21.

Orange Butter ▶

½ cup butter or margarine
2 teaspoons fresh orange juice
1 teaspoon snipped fresh
  parsley
1 clove garlic, cut in half
½ teaspoon grated orange peel
⅛ teaspoon salt
⅛ teaspoon dried tarragon
  leaves
3 to 4 drops hot pepper sauce

About ½ cup

In 2-cup measure, combine all
ingredients. Microwave at 70%
(Medium High) for 1½ minutes.
Stir. Microwave at 70% (Medium
High) for 30 seconds to 1 minute,
or until hot and bubbly. Stir.
Remove garlic. Serve warm
with seafood.

Lemon Butter: Follow recipe
above, substituting lemon juice
for orange juice. Substitute
lemon peel for orange peel.

Quick & Easy Marinade

2 tablespoons vegetable oil
½ cup thinly sliced celery
2 tablespoons chopped onion
⅛ teaspoon celery seed
¼ teaspoon grated orange peel
2 to 4 drops sesame oil
  (optional)
¾ cup apple juice
1 tablespoon sugar
1 tablespoon cider vinegar

About 1 cup

In 1-quart casserole, combine
oil, celery, onion, celery seed,
orange peel and sesame oil.
Cover. Microwave at High for
1 to 1½ minutes, or until celery
and onion are tender-crisp. Stir
in remaining ingredients. Microwave, uncovered, at High for
2 to 2½ minutes, or just until
mixture begins to boil. Cool
slightly. Pour over fish fillets.
Cover. Chill for 1 hour to
marinate. Remove fish from
marinade. Microwave as
directed on page 21.

Apricot Butter

¼ cup butter or margarine
2 tablespoons sliced green
  onion
¾ teaspoon dry mustard
¼ teaspoon ground ginger
2 tablespoons packed brown
  sugar
1 can (8¾ oz.) apricot halves,
  drained and chopped

About ¾ cup

In 1-quart casserole, combine
butter, onion, mustard and
ginger. Cover. Microwave at
High for 1½ to 2 minutes, or
until onion is tender, stirring
once. Stir in brown sugar and
apricots. Microwave at High
for 1½ to 2½ minutes, or until
mixture boils, stirring after every
minute. Serve with fish fillets
or chicken.

Shrimp Butter

½ cup butter or margarine
1 tablespoon sliced green
  onion
1 tablespoon snipped fresh
  parsley
¼ teaspoon dried tarragon
  leaves
1 tablespoon fresh lemon juice
1 can (4¼ oz.) tiny shrimp,
  rinsed and drained

About ½ cup

In 1-quart casserole, combine
butter, onion, parsley and
tarragon. Microwave at High for
1½ to 3 minutes, or until butter
melts and onion is tender. Stir
in remaining ingredients. Serve
with fish.

Tangy Dijon Butter

6 tablespoons butter or
  margarine
1 tablespoon lemon juice
2 teaspoons Dijon mustard
½ teaspoon onion powder
¼ teaspoon salt
⅛ teaspoon pepper

About ½ cup

In 2-cup measure, combine all
ingredients. Microwave at 70%
(Medium High) for 1½ to 2½
minutes, or until mixture can be
stirred smooth. Stir vigorously
with fork to blend. Let stand for
3 to 5 minutes to thicken slightly.
Serve over fish, seafood or
chicken breasts.

Almond-Caper Butter

⅓ cup butter or margarine
½ cup sliced almonds
⅛ teaspoon garlic powder
⅛ teaspoon paprika
2 tablespoons snipped fresh
  parsley
1 tablespoon capers, drained
1 tablespoon fresh lemon juice

About ⅔ cup

Place butter in 9-inch round
baking dish. Microwave at High
for 1 to 2 minutes, or until butter
melts. Stir in almonds, garlic
powder and paprika. Microwave
at High for 4 to 5 minutes, or
until almonds are lightly browned,
stirring after every minute. Stir in
remaining ingredients. Serve
over fish fillets.

Basting Butter ▶

½ cup butter or margarine
1 tablespoon sliced green
  onion
1 tablespoon snipped fresh
  parsley
1 clove garlic, minced
⅛ teaspoon paprika
2 tablespoons grated
  Parmesan cheese

½ cup

In 4-cup measure, combine
butter, onion, parsley, garlic and
paprika. Microwave at High for
2 to 3 minutes, or until butter
melts. Stir in Parmesan cheese.
Brush on fish or chicken.

Dill Basting Butter: Follow
recipe above, substituting dried
dill weed for paprika.

Citrus Basting Butter: Follow
recipe above, substituting
¼ teaspoon grated lemon, lime
or orange peel for paprika.

Index